PARABLES

The Arrows of God

———— ■ ————

Megan McKenna

ORBIS BOOKS

Maryknoll, New York 10545

The Catholic Foreign Mission Society of America (Maryknoll) recruits and trains people for overseas missionary service. Through Orbis Books, Maryknoll aims to foster the international dialogue that is essential to mission. The books published, however, reflect the opinions of their authors and are not meant to represent the official position of the society.

Queries regarding rights and permissions should be addressed to: Orbis Books, P. O. Box 308, Maryknoll, New York 10545-0308.

Published by Orbis Books, Maryknoll, NY 10545-0308
Manufactured in the United States of America

Unless otherwise noted, biblical translations are from the *Christian Community Bible*, 8th edition (Claretian Publications, 1991) and have been edited for inclusive language.

Library of Congress Cataloging-in-Publication Data

McKenna, Megan.
    Parables : the arrows of God / Megan McKenna.
      p. cm.
    ISBN 0-88344-975-7 (paper)
    1. Jesus Christ—Parables—Meditations.   2. Bible. N.T.—
Parables—Meditations.   I. Title.
    BT375.2.M33 1994
    226.8'06—dc20

                        94-16333
                          CIP

For Lambert Joseph Luna
an arrow and apprentice to John the Baptist
and friend of God
who taught me how to sharpen the arrow
bend the bow
and send it home to the hearts of folk
with grace and style.

With gratitude and affection.

Contents

Introduction

————— ■ —————

For many of us, the most familiar parts of scripture are the parables that Jesus used in his teaching. To Jesus' audiences, the parables covered common ground; the people knew about sheep and shepherds, lost coins, vineyards, unjust judges, wayward children. The parables were easy for his hearers to relate to, because they dealt with practical, down-to-earth matters.

The parables are easy for us too, at least on the surface. We've heard them for years. Given the title, most of us can tell the story. We know the tale of the prodigal son, the one lost sheep, the seed that fell on good ground, and all the rest. But we may need to hear these meaning-filled and provocative stories again and again. When we open our ears and our hearts, we may indeed end up acknowledging that for all our familiarity with the parables, we have never really heard them before, never understood them, never taken them into our hearts.

The fact is that these seemingly simply stories are multifaceted views into inner truth and reality. They provoke the basic questions: What is our treasure? What kind of ground do we provide for the seed? What price are we willing to pay for the kingdom? Often they turn on a turn of phrase, one pivotal point. And they seldom end as we would expect— or in a way that allows us to be comfortable with ourselves.

We need to keep the reality reflected in the parables before us. And we don't have to get too psychological, spiritual, personal—or even theological—to understand the reality of these stories. We do need open ears and open minds and open hearts. For the parables don't simply recount a clever tale. They start out that way, grounded in the most commonplace experiences and locations, but then they jerk the rug from under us, turning our world upside down and challenging some of our basic assumptions about ourselves, our neighbors, our world, our God. They grab our hearts and minds and twist them into a new position, a fresh awareness. And ultimately, of course, the insights and enlightenment they provide encourage us—drive us!—to change our way of being human, of being Christian.

The parables are all about justice and mercy. The two are entwined in Jesus' revelation of the kingdom of his Father. They reveal the truth of the heavenly reign and challenge us to live in the now of that kingdom, the now we know in one special way in the least of our brothers and sisters. Jesus is adamant on the Father's option for the poor. The parables are prophetic and demanding. They call us to conversion and humility—and acknowledgment that we are given much and must return much, that our lives belong to the kingdom and to God, practiced in our sharing with others.

Parables draw us in, softly and with subtlety. Then they hit us with the sledge hammer of revelation. They are revolutionary, subverting reality and undermining the existing structures and systems and relationships and attitudes—all the trappings of the status quo that keep the least among us in slavery and without hope while we look the other way, choosing to be oblivious to their claim upon us. "Listen, you who have ears to hear."

Parables point to the kingdom. They are, indeed, the "arrows of God." They pierce us and make us painfully aware of our need to change the way we relate to ourselves, others, and God. We look—and we see. This is how we must live in God's kingdom. We are called, and know ourselves called.

When we understand the function of the parable as an arrow of God, we can hear anew the ancient scriptural story of a living parable, John the Baptist, who foreshadowed the Father's brightest arrow of all, our guide to the kingdom,

Jesus. The words of Isaiah apply with equal promise to these arrows of the Father: "He made me into a polished arrow set apart in his quiver" (Isaiah 49:1-2). So it is fitting that a book about the parables begin with John, the first arrow, who called his people to repentance and preparation. What does John say to us today?

And, of course, after John comes Jesus, the ultimate arrow of God, telling his stories and calling us through the ages to "come, follow me." Jesus tells parables to break through our deafness, our hardness of heart. And then he gives us himself, the clearest parable of the Father. But that is where we will end, with Jesus, the Arrow—and the Archer.

What kind of parable are we? What can we become? Perhaps the answer is in a story.

■ Once upon a time there was a king who ruled a small kingdom. It wasn't great, and it wasn't really known for any of its resources or people. But the king did have a diamond, a great perfect diamond that had been in his family for generations. He kept it on display for all to see and appreciate. People came from all over the country to admire it and gaze at it.

Soon the word of it spread to neighboring countries, and more people came to look at it. Soon the people felt that the diamond was theirs; somehow it gave them a sense of pride, of dignity, of worth. Then one day a soldier came to the king with the news that, although no one had touched the diamond, for it was guarded night and day, the diamond was cracked. The king ran to see, and sure enough there was a crack right through the middle of the diamond.

Immediately he summoned all the jewelers of the land and had them look at the diamond. One after another they examined the diamond and gave the bad news to the king: the diamond was useless; it was irredeemably flawed. The king was crushed, so were the people. Somehow they felt they had lost everything.

Then out of nowhere came an old man who claimed to be a jeweler. He asked to see the diamond. After examining it, he looked up and confidently told the king, "I can fix it. In fact, I can make it better than it was before." The king was shocked and a bit leery. The old man said, "Give me the jewel, and in a week I'll bring it back fixed." Now the king was not about to let the stone out of his sight, even if it *was* ruined, so he gave the old man a room, all the tools and food and drink he needed and he waited. The whole kingdom waited. It was a long week.

At the end of the week the old man appeared with the stone in his hand and gave it to the king. The king couldn't believe his eyes. It was magnificent. The old man had fixed it, and he had made it even better than it was before! He had used the crack that ran through the middle of the stone as a stem and carved an intricate, full-blown rose, leaves, and thorns into the diamond. It was exquisite.

The king was overjoyed and offered the old man half his kingdom. He had taken something beautiful and perfect and improved upon it! But the old man refused in front of everyone, saying, "I didn't do that at all. What I did was to take something flawed and cracked at its heart and turn it into something beautiful."

That is, of course, the only thing any of us can ever hope to do: take something that is cracked and flawed at its heart and turn it into a diamond rose for God. But we must remember that someone else carves us and that we are meant to do the same for strangers, neighbors and friends so that there will be a bouquet of roses at the end of time.

1

The First Arrow–John the Baptist

———— ■ ————

Listen to me, O islands,
pay attention, peoples from distant lands.
Yahweh called me from my mother's womb;
he pronounced my name before I was born.
He made my mouth like a sharpened sword.
He hid me in the shadow of his hand.
He made me into a polished arrow
set apart in his quiver (Isaiah 49:1-2).

Isaiah speaks of one who is the servant of Yahweh, one who will gather the remnant of the people. This description can be either of Jesus the suffering servant, or of John the Baptizer, the cousin and forerunner of Jesus the prophet. It is often used for the feast of John, June 24.

In Mark's gospel we see this prophet-preacher who makes his appearance in the desert, warning the people and announcing the necessity of a baptism of repentance for the forgiveness of sins. He is the messenger of advent, of the long-awaited one hidden in the midst of the people, hidden in God's quiver. John, the first arrow, is out and on its way, straight to the heart of the people of Israel and all peoples who wait for hope, for transformation and the good news of God baptizing us with the Spirit, with fire and truth. And people come from the country of Judea and even from the city of Jerusalem to confess their sins in the River Jordan. But even as John baptizes them he is clear, "After me there will come one who is mightier than I am; I have baptized you with water, but he will baptize you in the Holy Spirit. As for me, I am not worthy to bend down and untie his sandals" (Mark 1:7-8).

This is John, and Isaiah's reading can be called John's Magnificat, the praise of God through John's life, just as Mary's Magnificat is praise of God through her life. Isaiah begins with a lengthy description of John and how God sees him—as a polished arrow. The immediacy, once loosed and set free, cannot be retrieved, brought back. John points, even when not in motion. Look! He points to another, to Jesus, to the Lamb of God, and he sends his own disciples away, after the one he points out (John 1). Until the moment John appears, he has been hidden in the quiver of God, in the desert, but perhaps more hidden in the heart of God. God uses John the way an archer uses an arrow, to pierce the hearts of the hunted. God hunts his people Israel with the force and directedness of John, with an arrow sent straight to the heart of people, to call them to repentance. A sharp sword or arrow, when honed, can go straight through to the bone with no pain until afterward. It reveals, opens up. John will be that laying bare for Israel. His words and actions will cut straight through flesh and bone with clarity and sureness and only afterward will the pain of that revelation be felt.

Two individuals who feel the pain and react to it with anger and violence are Herod and his ill-chosen wife and queen, Herodias, the ex-wife of his brother Philip. The woman holds a grudge against John, a lethal and deadly grudge, and waits for her time, a time to trap her husband Herod, who respects and fears John, into killing him. At Herod's birthday party she arranges for her daughter Salome to dance for him, and he rashly promises to give her anything she wants. And what she wants, obeying her mother's orders, is John's head, on a plate. And so the arrow, the word that set in motion a new testament, a new hope for the people, is murdered at a dinner party. His life is worth the price of a dance.

This prophet is a light to the nations, a last flare in the long dark, and for a moment the earth is illumined. All the world is seen for what it is, in the way a flash of lightning tears across the sky at night and for just that moment reveals everything. Early in the gospel of Luke there are questions about this manchild, this prophet whose birth is heralded by an angel and his father's muteness and disbelief. He is born of elderly parents on the outskirts of Jerusalem. What will this child be? Even his neighbors and his parents' friends believe that the hand of the Lord is upon him, with him even from birth and before (Luke 1:66). Before birth, in his mother's womb, he is singled out and called. The Japanese call this moment a person's "original face," as God created and formed the person and called him into being. John is named. Without a word his very presence loosed the voice of his father to cry out and praise God in the song-prayer we call the Benedictus. The very announcement of who he is sets Zachariah free. John's marvelous birth is a portent of the power to come to him.

Yet the power of John is nothing in comparison to the one to come: Jesus, his cousin. John is born of an old barren woman in the usual human ways, but Jesus is born of a young virgin without sexual intervention. This is the way prepared for the new creation, where nothing will be impossible. It prepares us to believe in the resurrection of this child, once destroyed by others. These others, those who do not believe in dreams and portents, seek from the very beginning to kill both children. Eventually they succeed, only to be tripped up by God.

John teaches us the art of faith-dancing. We first meet him in an announcement, "And you, my child, shall be called prophet of the Most High, for you shall go before the Lord to prepare the way for him" (Luke 1:76). He dances before God, as David danced before the ark in worship and delight at the presence of the Lord hidden in the midst of the people; for when Mary with Jesus in her womb comes to visit his mother Elizabeth, he stirs. This is the one he points to, and he kicks and leaps in recognition and begins the dance of the new kingdom of the meek and the humble and the poor. The dance begins with an old woman, a young girl, and two yet-to-be born children on a hill outside Jerusalem. As John grows up, he dances off to the desert to live hidden in the hand of God, hidden in God's quiver. When John makes his appearance and preaches a new way of living—the turn-around dance step—he lures others into the waters of the Jordan, into the waters of baptism. He dances the prophet's and leader's dance much as many folk dance down aisles in church to come to the altar and commit themselves to hope, to a fresh start, to a new life of grace and freedom with others.

Jesus will take up this dance and will give John, in prison, another series of steps in the dance. When John is jailed, he sends his disciples to Jesus with a question, "Are you the one who is to come or should we expect someone else?" (Matthew 11:3). John is this arrow of God sent ahead to pre-pare the way, and yet in the shadows of death and despair he questions. This Jesus, this preacher who has picked up his mantle of justice and is calling people to freedom and liberation, is not what he expected. The arrow does not know the target or the hand that set it loose! But Jesus is clear with John. He sends back the disciples with words from which John will take heart, words to heed and ponder in his jail cell, the words from the prophet Isaiah, "The blind see, the lame walk, the lepers are made clean, the deaf hear, the dead are brought back to life and good news is reaching the poor. And well it is for the one who does not take offense at me" (Matthew 11:4-6).

Then Jesus turns to the crowds and announces that John is the one the prophets spoke about as the messenger, the one sent ahead to scout the way and prepare a path in the desert for the dreamer who was to come. Jesus declares,

> "I tell you this; never has a greater prophet than John the Baptist appeared, and yet the least in the kingdom of Heaven is greater than he. . . . The time of the Proph-ets and the Law extends up to John. It was the time of prophecy and if you accept their message, John is this Elijah, whose coming was predicted. If anyone has ears to hear, let him listen" (Matthew 11:11, 13-15).

John is the first parable, the first surprise, the first and the greatest in the old ways and the least in the new paths to peace and justice. In this kingdom whose king John is not worthy to bend before and offer homage to or even untie his sandals, the greatest is the least, the poor, the sheep, the lost child and coin, the widow's mite, the old woman mother, the lowly virgin, the dangerous children. These are the prophets of the testament of Jesus, the words of hope, the flesh and blood of justice. Even John's work and world are turned upside down and inside out. In prison, this parable of freedom from sin and evil learns what liberation will be. The arrow is no longer needed, for the archer, the one who wields the double-edged sword of tender regard and justice, is no longer hidden in the quiver of God but present in the people's midst. Hope has come, and the intimations of incarnation, of life's strength in the face of murder and unnecessary death and resurrection, are here. These are Jesus' words to John; they comfort him in prison. The new steps in the dance are being tried out in the cities and towns of Judea.

And so John's life ends with a dance, one of the old dances of power and intrigue and dishonesty and rage, and John loses his head. Another dances for the old regime of kings and queens and politics and sex for power, and John, the dancer, is dead. This parable, this first twist of the new times asks us if we dance for the kingdom. Do we dance for preparation, for justice and hope, for Jesus and the Spirit, or do we dance for another in power?

John is the least in the kingdom of Jesus, because he recognizes Jesus but does not know him. He sends others to Jesus to ask if he is the one. John must change his mind about Jesus and trust in him, believing that he is the one long awaited. John dies, with his death forcing Jesus' hand and moving him into the forefront. John lives and dies passionately devoted to only one thing: being the polished arrow, the sharpened sword of the Lord held in his hand, used to change the direction of history, to focus attention on another, and to stir all fears attached to power and might. John lives to bring change, altercations, and to rekindle a hope that had died into ashes.

I once watched in fascination, awe and near terror as a friend, a Native American, took down a deer with one arrow. It thrust through skin, flesh, sinew and bone. The arrow had been polished until it was razor sharp. Suddenly I knew John the Baptist—his power, his meaning, his utter singularity and singleheartedness, the very strength of God gathered, loosed, unleashed into the world and set at us. We, the people of God, were and are the target, targeted for repentance, for justice, for the maturation of the Spirit, for hope.

John, the arrow, the first parable of Jesus' reign, asks, "At whom are we aimed? To whose heart are we sent? Who is aiming at ours? What are we meant to be? For whom are we kept by God? When is our time to be launched into history and the hope of the poor? Where are the arrows concealed and hidden now?" John, this arrow, was hidden in the mind of God for generations, then in his old mother's womb for nine months, then in the desert of Israel and lastly in a jail cell. This arrow, this man, was named by God before birth, wrested away from kin, family, blood ties, belonging only to earth, to history and the fullness of time, born only to turn and face the Christ, even in his womb, recognizing him and rising up and dancing.

There is a grand poem from the black tradition simply titled "John."

> somebody coming in blackness
> like a star
> and the world be a great bush
> on his head
> and his eyes be fire
> in the city
> and his mouth be true as time
>
> he be calling the people brother
> even in the prison
> even in the jail
>
> i'm just only a baptist preacher
> somebody bigger than me coming
> in blackness like a star (Lucille Clifton)

Nietzsche once said, "Only those who can contain within themselves the pressure and the chaos of tension can give birth to a dancing star." John the Baptist teaches us all to live with that pressure and chaos and give birth to the light of the world. John, the arrow, the dancer, the child who goes before the Lord with words of repentance and forgiveness and wild fire, the prophet of hope and what is to come, is the parable of preparation. Nothing is as it appears to be, and nothing will ever be the same. John is a practice parable to get us used to the stories that Jesus will tell.

Come now, it's time to practice being taken off guard, questioned, being taught new dance steps, playing "hot potato" and finding out we're the potatoes who will fall finally into the outstretched arms of God.

2

Seeking the Treasure

———— ■ ————

■ Once upon a time there were two groups of battleships on maneuvers. The weather was terrible, pea soup fog, high winds and seas. The second night out was worse. The captain stood the bridge all night, wary of just second-hand reports. He didn't want to chance the battleships of the other group colliding with them in the open seas. All night he checked on the night sky and what could be seen. Toward dawn the officer yelled, "Light on the starboard side, sir!" The captain yelled back, "Is she steady or moving?" A pause and the reply, "Sir, she's steady!" "Send a message ASAP," he roared. "Change course 20 degrees immediately." The message was relayed and sent. Then back came a reply on the radio that was passed on to the captain, "Sir, they suggest you change course." The captain was furious. He turned and yelled, "You tell them I am a captain and I'm ordering them to change course, 20 degrees hard now. Don't those fools know we are on a collision course?" The message was sent. Then the reply came back. "I'm an ensign second class, and I suggest you change course now." The captain was near spitting, and the light was fast approaching. "Damn it, you tell them I'm the captain of a battleship and they'd better obey my orders immediately!" The message was sent. Back came the reply, "I'm a lighthouse." And the battleship turned.

When I tell this story as an introduction to parables everyone laughs. Why? The tension builds up and then breaks, granting a release in laughter. Stories always bring us to a point—it can be relief, laughter or tears, or insight.

One of the reasons we laugh at stories is because they are about us, and our laughter says that we acknowledge that they are really about us. We can be the captain of the battleship, the communications officer, the ensign or the lighthouse. Our vantage point reveals the story as we heard it. And they are different stories depending on our point of view. Different stories altogether. Their hearing can validate their reality, and the tables can be turned.

After we hear a lot of stories, we begin to get crafty and ask: Where is this going? What is this saying? Who is being put in his place? This is what is happening in the church today. We are, many of us, used to hearing the stories of Jesus, of the church, of the kingdom, from the same point of view. Where we stand in the story determines what we hear. But since the Vatican Council the Spirit has been working very hard among a specific group of people—the poor—who hear the stories of scripture from another vantage point. The good news to the poor, the heart of the gospel, is being heard differently. The stories are the same, but the hearing is different. In the last thirty-five years the church has been listening to the stories through the ears and the interpretations of the poor.

The poor, those who make up the majority of believers in the church, in Latin America, in Africa and in other third-world countries, have been interpreting their lives and the scriptures. We are hearing the stories anew.

The reality is that Jesus' stories call for change. We all need change, massive radical change and conversion. By our baptisms we pledge constant conversion, alone and together with other believers in the community of church. The stories of Jesus call us to change, just as they call believers in every generation and geography to change, to follow Jesus more closely and truly. They are inspired; the Spirit put power into the words to evoke us, to call us forth to change, as individuals in community. Every time we hear the scriptures and we don't change, we haven't really heard.

Inspiration—we hear and we change. Do we? How often have we heard the scriptures and how *much* have we changed? Is it noticeable year to year? Do we learn more of compassion, alter the way we make moral decisions, practice more justice and work for peace? Do we live more simply and care more for the poor, shift our understanding and behavior toward our neighbors? Perhaps if our changes aren't noticeable, we are not changing. Hearing means changing. It is our call as baptized believers.

Our primary value is constant conversion: look more like Jesus, act more like Jesus, and become more like Jesus together, in the context of the Trinity. We are Jesus in the world, and we are the only Jesus most people are ever going to meet. The incarnation says God became human, and being human is the way we understand what it means to be like our God. Matthew's gospel says: "Truly, I say to you: whenever you did this to one of the least, to my brothers and sisters, you did it to me" (Matthew 25:40). The criterion for our religion is incarnation. The way we act toward one another is the way we act toward God. A prayer of St. Teresa of Avila reminds us: the only feet God has on earth are ours; the only hands God has on earth are ours; the only heart and mind God has on earth are our own hearts and minds. Do we act like Jesus with each other?

We must constantly change to become more of what we proclaim to be. The people sitting next to us may not be just what they appear to be—they may be the only Jesus we will meet face to face. If this is true, then what we do to each other is absolutely crucial; it is what we do to God. And what we don't do to each other, we don't do to God, and God will take that personally all our lives. Most of us say we believe this, but we don't spend our lives making this story of incarnation come true.

■ Once upon a time Nasrudin lost his donkey, and he ran through the village streets yelling and crying, "My donkey is missing. There is a reward for finding him. Anyone who finds him can have my donkey for himself!" People listened and started laughing at him. Nasrudin was again being crazy and insane, even stupid. Finally someone stopped him and told him how stupid he sounded. But

Nasrudin turned and eyed him carefully and said: "I am not crazy, sir. It is you who do not see or undersand. If someone finds the donkey that I have grown to care for because of its service to me, and I give it away as reward for the finding, then I can do two things that will give me great pleasure. I will find something treasured that was lost, and I will take great delight in giving away as a gift something that I value highly." And Nasrudin walked off leaving the other man silenced and in thought.

Most of Jesus' stories begin with "The kingdom of God is like" or "The reign of God is like." What is this kingdom, this reign? Let's listen to one of the shortest stories of Jesus about this kingdom of God, this reign:

■ *"If you have ears, then hear. The kingdom of Heaven is like a treasure hidden in a field. The man who finds it buries it again; and so happy is he, that he goes and sells everything he has, so that he may buy that field" (Matthew 13:43-45).*

This is a strange story, mysterious. It makes us uneasy. Our minds go in a hundred different directions. The Spirit stirs us up. The Spirit stirs the waters of baptism, blows where it will, stirs the air, makes a loud noise when it comes upon the disciples in the upper room. If the story makes us uneasy, then the Spirit is near, hovering, getting ready to cry "Gotcha!"

Or we may feel "guilty." "He went and sold all he had and bought that field" stirs guilt. How many of us have sold everything we have to buy that field? Do we own nothing but the field? If we ever meet someone who has done this, we know we have met someone the world does not know what to do with, someone who has the kingdom, the treasure! Guilt is good. It warns us that we have either done something we shouldn't have done, or we haven't done something we should have done. Guilt is only bad when we collect it over long periods of time and don't do anything with it.

We need to be attentive to what the parable might be trying to say. We need to hear it again, and again, to open a door and acknowledge that we may not ever have really heard it, understood it, or have ever taken it to heart. This story provokes basic questions, such as "What is the treasure?" No matter how many times you hear the story or answer this question, you still wonder about it. There is some sort of shift of priorities going on in the story—the man is going to sell all that he has so he can buy the field, but why does he go and hide the treasure again? He buries it again to guarantee ownership. The one who owns the field owns the treasure.

All the parables are very practical and down to earth. They deal with economics, politics, everyday occurrences, violence, work, relationships. We need to keep that in mind and not get too psychological, spiritual, personal or theological before we understand the reality of the story. A small piece of information is the pivot point of the story. The man buries the treasure again. Then he sells everything in order to get the treasure that is still buried in the field. What are we willing to give up for this treasure? If we really want the kingdom of heaven, what will we give up? This is a question that does not brook any easy answers.

This one person sold all his possessions. He knew what the treasure was, and so he was willing to give up everything else. Do we know what the treasure is? Does knowing make us more willing to give up what is necessary to buy the field? What is the risk involved? What is our experience of the kingdom? Or are we missing something?

Parables frustrate us. They make us feel we may be missing something crucial. Jesus is frustrated that people listening to him won't make choices, won't decide, won't act on what they hear, and so he resorts to a form of teaching that ups the frustration for everyone who listens. We were given the treasure at baptism. What have we done with it? Most of us have buried it back in the field where we found it. We haven't done much rejoicing, publicly or privately, and we haven't sold everything to make sure we can buy the field. We figure that because we know where it is, it is ours. But this parable is one of finding, and so we must begin by looking. We must learn to seek, and when we find what we are looking for, we must put it back where we found it, go home and change, and then be willing to sell all we have for the one important thing. It is a pattern Jesus will repeat again and again. In fact, the next two verses are another parable:

■ *"Again, the kingdom of Heaven is like a trader who is looking for fine pearls. Once he has found a pearl of exceptional quality, he goes away, sells everything he has and buys it"* (Matthew 13:45-46).

He found the pearl of great price! He sold everything to obtain it. The pattern is the same. What are we looking for? Where do we find it? What do we do with it? And what are we going to do to make sure we've secured it?

Jesus' stories require hard things of us. We think of who we are in the kingdom: children of the king. We hold a place of privilege and responsibility. We are heirs. We want the kingdom, but we don't want to pay the going price. We want it now, not later. And we don't want any pain involved in claiming our inheritance. We want the privileged relationship of the favored son or daughter, but we don't want the responsibility and the hard work of keeping the kingdom together.

But how does the kingdom come? As for Jesus, it comes through living, through picking up our cross, through crucifixion, death and resurrection. The kingdom comes in our lives, in the world through the way of the cross, the way of justice and truth, the way of speaking hope to others.

This story is closely tied to other pieces of the good news, especially the parable of the pharisee and the person who went home justified for his prayer and worship in the synagogue. This is followed closely by the story of Zacchaeus, the tax collector who is justified and saved by meeting Jesus. Zacchaeus is a short man. He wants to see Jesus, so he climbs a tree to get a better view. Jesus stops under the tree and says, "Come on down, I'm having dinner at your house tonight." As Zacchaeus climbs down, everyone around starts to murmur, "He's going to the house of a public sinner and is going to eat with him." How do we feel about that? Imagine a person today who is notorious. How would we feel about Jesus going to that person's house for dinner if it were Madonna or Sinaid O'Connor?

This story reveals the criteria for baptism in Luke's community. Before baptism, a person had to do justice fourfold and then take half of all he or she owned and give it to the poor, just as Zacchaeus did. Then the person could say "Our Father," could sit down at the table of the Lord with the community and together call God "Our Father." If that were the criteria for baptism today, who would be getting baptized? What if every year at the renewal of our baptismal promises at the Easter Vigil, we couldn't participate until we had done justice fourfold for everything in the past year and had taken half of everything we had and given it to the poor? What would such a parish be like? What would the world be like if the universal church did this? Certainly the quality of life would be very different. There would be a great deal of joy, and I suspect that many people would be able to see the kingdom of heaven very clearly. Some people might be poorer, but many people would be much better off. There would be a real sense of being brothers and sisters with Jesus, children of God, all beloved, living in community. Everyone would know that something was going on in the church. That's the kingdom of heaven.

Many of us don't like this vision. We are afraid that if we give up all our stuff, we'll end up on the streets. But the story says that we should give up half our possessions after we do what is just and right, what is human. This is the kingdom of heaven. This is why the good news affected people the way it did in the early church community, and is why it drew forth a response of real conversion.

We are supposed to be living the kingdom of heaven now, more and more and more each day, so that people can rejoice exceedingly when they meet us and say, "They have found the treasure!" Then they will be willing to go home and sell everything they have so that they too can be sure to find the treasure. The treasure is the relationship with God revealed and expressed in community of believers, between God and God's people, the presence of Jesus in the community. We really must do what we say: "May your kingdom come, may your will be done on earth as it already is in heaven." God's will—"I have come that they may have life, life in all its fullness" (John 10:10).

We pray the words, but when we think about putting them into practice, we think "You've got to be kidding." So Jesus told stories, parables to get the idea, the dream, across to people just like us. We don't need to think about making ourselves destitute, but we do need to start thinking about giving away what we don't use, or don't need, to people who do need it—after we do justice, what is required of all of us. And then we need to make sure that everyone we are in relation with, or connected to, or know of, is treated justly. How can we be in a right relationship with God if we are not in a right relationship with our brothers and sisters? If God has become human and dwells among us, then our God lurks hidden in the people all around us, close at hand. It's all of a piece—concrete, demanding, calling us to conversion.

The gospel is spelled out clearly and precisely in the parables and tales of individuals. Mark and Matthew include the story of the rich young man who approaches Jesus. Jesus looks at him with love and invites him into discipleship, but the young man turns down the invitation and goes away because the requirements are too hard. "Go, sell what you have and give the money to the poor, and you will have riches in heaven. Then come and follow me" (Mark 10:21). What if he had said yes? There would have been a thirteenth disciple. But he walked away.

There is nothing wrong with being rich, except that it gets in the way of the coming of the kingdom of heaven. If there are rich then there are poor. If there are very rich, then there are very poor. Wealth gets in the way of justice and the kingdom of heaven, because it separates us from God and from our brothers and sisters in need. The United Nations defines *rich* today as having more than is needed to survive. How much do we need to survive? What is the quality of life that is practiced, encouraged and subscribed to in the kingdom of heaven and by those who have found the treasure?

This parable begins with a command: "If you have ears, then hear!" We wouldn't be studying the scriptures if we didn't have some experience of the treasure, of the kingdom, and if we did not think of ourselves as Jesus' disciples. We have found the treasure, although we may not know what it is, or we may have stolen it and not bought the field. We may not have ever rejoiced in it or been able to point out where we discovered it. But we have found the treasure. We have been in the field long enough to have glimpsed it.

So what do we do with the treasure once we've found it? The line that stumps most people is, "he went and hid it again." Why not just take it and run? After all, he found it. But what about the owners of the field? How would they feel later when they find that someone—we—took their treasure, their property? Furious, annoyed, stolen from, cheated—all those feelings surface from their point of view. What if God feels the same way when we find the treasure and run away with it, never acknowledging whose treasure it is, to whom it belongs?

Surely God put the treasure there for us to find! Does our God want us, as individuals, to get the treasure, or does God, Jesus' God, want us to find the treasure and take the field as well? We want the treasure, but often we don't want the field. It all depends on what the field is—and what the treasure is! The treasure and the field—these are two halves of the kingdom of God, and to have only one half is not to know the kingdom.

The treasure and the field: what are they? Let's look at the treasure first. This treasure is the reign of God, the kingdom of heaven, so God and heaven have something to do with each other, and kingdom and reign, authority and power are in there somehow. As we talk about the meaning of the reign of God and the kingdom of heaven, we begin to realize that our worlds are small, enclosed and confined; we need each other to hear, to see and to know what is hidden in the text. If God is a trinity, a community, God likes us to talk these things over with each other and come to clearer insights. The truth is always easier to see with others; then it is not hindered by our own perceptions. Answers about the kingdom abound, usually including Jesus and love.

But what does Jesus teach and talk about all the time? His Father, his God: "Our Father," "that we all may be one as the Father is one." Jesus does the will of his Father so that his Father's kingdom may come on earth. We have to move beyond Jesus to the Father. Jesus is an arrow pointing to the Father; we can't stay with the arrow. We must get to the Fa-

ther. We may have wrapped our lives around Jesus, but it is
the power of the Spirit that sends the arrow to the Father. We
follow Jesus, and Jesus' way is the way to the Father. Jesus'
relationship to the Father is the core of his life and preaching. He is the child of God. In baptism we are given this same
relationship. We become children of God. Baptism gives us
the relationship, gives us the treasure.

Child of God—how old is your mother? Are you an old
child? We think of children of two, three or four years who
need and want to be taken care of, tended. But Jesus grew
up as a child of God, a grown, mature child. We don't always grow up in relation to God. If we take the treasure and
run out of the field, then we remain a child of two, three or
four years. It is a young child who finds something and says
"It's mine," and takes it. But we are supposed to grow up. In
Luke 2 we are told, "And Jesus grew in wisdom and age and
grace before God and the earth." We are supposed to be growing in the same way. As we do that, we hide the treasure
back in the field, learning to rejoice exceedingly and selling
all that we have and going back to buy the field, along with
the treasure.

What is this kingdom of heaven? Practically all of Jesus'
parables begin with, "The kingdom of heaven is like . . ." or
"The reign of God can be compared to . . ." What is it? We
might answer that it is a challenge, a confrontation. We could
say that the kingdom of heaven is what's left when we take
away our ego, our self-centeredness. Or the kingdom of
heaven is a perfect state of being, where there is no injustice,
no hunger, no want, no war. It is a place where our dreams
come true, a peace of mind, an attitude of being, twenty-
four hours a day of praising and glorying God. It's poverty
with great joy (very biblical). It's liberation. It's us, it's already here. It's our reward with Christ after living here, we
hope, because there are other options.

These first responses tell us that many people take the kingdom for granted, don't think about it too systematically, or
think of it in terms that we might reject or even find offen-
sive or severely limiting. And yet we pray for this kingdom
to come daily in the prayer Jesus taught to his disciples, "May
your kingdom come on earth as it is in heaven," and "May

your will be done, on earth now, as it is in heaven." For what are we praying? All of the above?

Jesus comes proclaiming the kingdom of heaven. The first words coming from Jesus in Mark's gospel are, "This is the time of fulfillment; the kingdom of God is at hand. Change your ways and believe the Good News" (Mark 1:15). The kingdom is close at hand. If we are asked to stick out our hand, we invariably extend it in front of us, as though to take something, to reach for something. We never think to reach out to the person beside us. It never enters our head. Yet this is how close the kingdom is to us, how close Jesus is to us. It's that close and that human.

We often make dichotomies between the kingdom of heaven *there* and the kingdom of heaven *here*. But whatever we say about the one to come, we can just as clearly posit about the one here in our midst now. If it isn't here, then it won't be there either. When the presence of Jesus is here, the kingdom is here. Through incarnation, the presence of God became human and dwelled among us, stayed among us with the kingdom. The kingdom of God is the presence of God with us here on earth in history.

What else is the treasure hidden in the field, the kingdom of God, besides this relationship? Have any of us had glimpses of heaven, been there momentarily? Yes. The kingdom is characterized by joy. When we live in joy, the virtue of joy, we live in the kingdom of God. A sense of joy, a fruit of the Spirit, precedes our selling all to buy the kingdom. Where do we put our joy? The person who finds the kingdom, this relationship, this treasure, rejoices exceedingly. What is it like for others when someone lives in joy? If all of us are living in joy, living in this adult relationship with Jesus and the Father, then there is peace. And there can be no peace without justice. The kingdom of God, then, is the kingdom of peace and justice. Not peace on an individual level that makes us feel good, but the peace that Jesus gives us. Even when we are being persecuted or made outcast, there is the sense of joy and peace that we are still living in the kingdom, that justice is being pursued and that peace is a reality. The treasure is the kingdom of peace and justice here on earth, now, not here in its fullness, but here.

St. Catherine of Siena says that for those who believe in Jesus, all the way home to heaven is heaven. Heaven is here on earth now. If we stumble on this treasure here on earth, if we stumble into this relationship, then we have stumbled into the kingdom of God. What would it be like to stumble into a place where we could experience this peace and justice here on earth? It would be a place where people were busy taking care of God's work, of God's people, a place of loving God instead of just taking care of themselves and their own people. This quality of who we are as believers says whether or not we are in the kingdom. Whom do we think about, whom do we worry about, who benefits from our decisions, our priorities and lives, our generosity and justice? If we are busy taking care of the kingdom of God, then God is busy taking care of us and our needs, just as with Jesus, his child. The kingdom of heaven is this relationship that Jesus had with the Father, extended now to us in the context of the community.

This relationship is built on trust, enormous amounts of trust, even in the face of rejection, persecution, loss of dreams—even the loss of Jesus' life, his betrayal by his disciples. The relationship is very intimate and close. Jesus knows God. It is a relationship of obedience, a relationship that expresses the compassion of God toward all others, with no picking and choosing of whom to care for and whom to befriend.

Chapter 5 of the gospel of John contains this gospel's only parable. In it Jesus describes himself as an apprentice, a disciple of the Father. He says, "My *Father* goes on working and so do I" (John 5:17). He is a watcher of the Father so that we in turn can watch him, imitate him and know what it's like to act like God. This is the relationship we are initiated into at baptism. We become the beloved children of God. In the gospels Jesus also hears the words, "This is my beloved child, in whom I am well pleased. Listen to him!" This is what God says about us, to us, "We are the beloved children of God, we are to listen to one another." In this relationship we are not primarily individual children, but children in relationship with our brothers and sisters, siblings, many, many of them, a huge group that we are drawn into. From baptism on, we are told to call God *"our* father," not *"my* father." Everything is communal.

So the kingdom of heaven has to do with community, for our God is community, the trinity. The image that most reflects trinity is community, and there is room in that relationship, that community, for everyone. Jesus' prayer at the Last Supper in John's gospel is that we all might be one, as the Father, the Child, and the Spirit are one. The kingdom is how this oneness is discovered, remembered, put back together again, experienced and shared in the world, in history. The kingdom is all of our relationships with God seen and known by others outside the community as well as by those within the believing group.

So that is the treasure. What of the field? The field is where the relationship is expressed, among people. The field is where we return the treasure we found. We hide it again, sell all that we have and go back and buy the field—move in with the folk. What does this mean? Change, each of us, all of us must change—individuals, religious communities, parishes, national churches. Even holiness has to be done together. This is a dream, the dream of God. Are we going to spend the rest of our lives making this dream come true? It is very hard, but full of grace. There is no rejecting of anyone else and nothing lacking in others. We fill up what is lacking in others, and they fill up what is lacking in us, like a great jigsaw puzzle being put together. It is a challenge, to be undertaken together. We are so often used to doing things *our* way, on our schedules. We must instead offer ourselves to others, do it *their* way, according to their needs, with whomever God presents to us in our daily lives.

The treasure is hidden in the field. The incarnation is hidden in people and in their needs and sorrows and hopes. Together the treasure is shared in the field. We can't just take the treasure for ourselves without community, without the world and the fact that we are responsible for each other. We enter the kingdom of heaven in its fullness because of what we have done for one another. Sometimes individuals can do very little in acts of charity, generosity, justice, but together we offer an alternative to the present reality. Together we can bring the kingdom. We are supposed to become the treasure hidden in the field, a new reality in the world, along with Jesus, and anyone who stumbles upon us will rejoice exceedingly and go therefore and sell everything they have to come back to the field, to us, and share the treasure.

■ Once upon a time there was a rabbi who loved the Torah. He was a very good preacher. Every Sabbath afternoon he could be found sitting in the backyard at his picnic table pouring over the texts for the following Sabbath service, preparing his sermon. Around him all his grandchildren and great grandchildren would be playing a game of hide and seek, a Sabbath afternoon ritual. They would scatter around, and he would hear them counting in the back of his mind: 1, 2, 3, 4, 5, 6, 7, 8, 9, 10, with squeals and laughter and running back and forth. He was used to it. One Sabbath afternoon he looked up, and there in front of him was one of his youngest grandchildren, no more than four or five, with tears running down his face, forlorn and unhappy. The man was a rabbi, but he was a grandfather first, and he stooped down and picked up his grandson and took him onto his lap, rocking him and asking him what was wrong. The little boy said,

"Grandfather, I love Sabbath afternoons, and I love to play hide and seek. It's my best game to play. All week long I look for hiding places. I wait all week to play the game with the big kids. I save my best place for Sabbath afternoon and I go hide. I've been sitting in my hiding place all afternoon. Nobody found me. But now they've decided to go play another game. They didn't even know I was still in my hiding place."

The rabbi dried the boy's tears and comforted him and finally sent him back to the others to play. He went back to his sermon, but he couldn't get his grandchild out of his mind. Finally he pushed the books and papers away and leaned back, folding his arms, and thought.

God, you are like my grandson. You find the best hiding places, and then on Sabbath you sit in your best hiding place and we don't find you, even when we look in the scriptures. You wait for us. Then we get tired and go off, leaving you crying.

That Sabbath he gave a completely different sermon.

God's favorite game, since the beginning of time, has been hide and seek. God finds us when we hide in all our best places, and we look for God, who hides in his best places. Until we find the God who hides and waits for us to find him, we will never know the joy of belonging to God, of finding God. Where does God hide? He hides in the United States. He hides in Ireland, in Waterford, in the two people who come to our front door. He hides in the person sitting next to us. He hides in the last place we would ever think to look for him, and he's there, probably weeping, still. Have we gone off to play another game?

■ Once upon a time there was an old man who lived on the outskirts of a town. He had lived there so long that no one knew who he was or where he had come from. Some said that once he had been very powerful, a king, but that was long ago. Others said, no, he was once very wealthy and generous, but without much now. Others said, no, he was wise and influential, and some even said he was holy. But the children just thought he was a stupid old man, and they made his life miserable. They threw stones at his windows, left dead cats on his doorstep, ripped up his garden, and shouted at him every chance they got.

Then one day an older boy came up with an idea to prove once and for all that their parents were wrong, that he wasn't wealthy, or once a king, or wise or holy, that he was just a stupid old man. He knew how to catch a bird in a snare. He told the other children that he would catch a bird, and together they'd go to the old man's house and knock on his door. When the man answered, he would ask him, "Old man, do you know what I have hidden behind my back?" Now, he might guess that it's a bird, but it's the second question that will get him. I'll ask him if the bird is dead or alive. If he says dead, then I'll just let the bird go free. If he answers that the bird is alive, then I'll just crush the bird to death in my hands. Either way, he's just a stupid old man.

The kids thought it was a great idea. The older boy caught the bird and off they went to the old man's house and rudely knocked on the door. The old man came to the door, looked around at all the children and knew they were up to something. The boy spoke quickly, "Old man, do you know what I have hidden behind my back?" The old man looked around at the children one by one and out of the corner of his eye he saw a white feather fall to the ground. He answered, "Yes, I do. It's a bird, a white bird." The children's eyes grew large. He could have guessed it was a bird, but how did he know it was white? Maybe their parents were right about him after all. But the leader was not to be deterred and quickly asked the second question. "Well, that was a good guess, but is the bird dead or alive?" Again, the old man looked around at each child, sadly, and finally his eyes came to rest on the older boy. He answered, "That all depends on you. The answer is in your hands."

A parable, contemporary or traditional or scriptural, causes stark and unexpected reactions. A parable causes an emotional response, evoking fear, loneliness, sorrow, horror, because the parable always throws the ending, the reality, the circumstances back into our lap. We react almost viscerally—"No, tell me what to do. No, it can't be. No, you don't mean. . . . Do I have to decide right now? Can we discuss this?" Whenever the truth hits us hard, it hits us in our stomach. That's why parables are often difficult to put on a page after you've heard the story, swallowed it and nearly choked on it.

Parables always go for the truth at the heart of the matter. In fact, every time we read the scriptures liturgically we can end by saying, "It all depends. The answer is in our hands." Whether or not the scriptures come true is up to us. Jesus came, proclaimed the good news, lived the good news, is the good news, and now he has entrusted the good news to us. If we don't make the good news come true in the world, then it dies. God trusts us a lot more than we would choose!

Sometimes we hear all the small details in a parable and fail to go for the heart of the matter. Is the story about the bird? How many animals were in the ark? We side-step the important point and hear the story from our limited and rather biased perceptions.

Often parables make us angry. There may be anger about others' behavior and attitudes. But, at root, we are angry at ourselves. The parable tells us the truth in some way about ourselves. Parables and the whole of scripture are truth-tellers. The text exposes us before ourselves and others.

Most of us want to be dealt with individually, not in a group, or classified as belonging to the human race or the various groups we are affiliated with. But parables and the gospels always say that we are all sinners, we are all in the same boat, and we have to look at this together because we either go down together or rise together. The parables of Jesus make us angry, sad, glad, nervous, because they tell us the truth about what we claim to be, even though the truth may not be apparent from our behavior, attitudes and alliances.

The parables do many things to us. But ultimately we want the stories to be good news. We want goodness, justice and right to triumph. In the tale above, we want the old man to triumph, even though he has to put up with a lot before he finally does. The role we take on in the story is always pivotal: the old man, the youth, the other children, the neighborhood, even the bird. The old man, the underdog, a respect for age, a sense of camaraderie because of exclusion, solitariness. We go for the one we are attracted to, that we think is like us, the one misjudged. We listen in the story for a glimpse of recognition.

Listeners can also be the bird, the nonhuman one, the helpless one, the victim, the one used by the others. Then there is the older boy, the one who is the center, pulling the attention, looking for status, power, proving his point. We can often hear this story, and others, from this point of view, but we don't admit to it readily. And there are the other children, just waiting to see what will happen, playing it safe, secure. The parables work like this.

■ There was a woman who wanted peace in the world and peace in her heart and all sorts of good things, but she was very frustrated. The world seemed to be falling apart. She would read the papers and get depressed. One day she decided to go shopping, and she went into a mall and picked a store at random. She walked in and was surprised to see Jesus behind the counter. She knew it was Jesus, because he looked just like the pictures she'd seen on holy cards and devotional pictures. She looked again and again at him, and finally she got up her nerve and asked, "Excuse me, are you Jesus?" "I am." "Do you work here?" "No," Jesus said, "I own the store." "Oh, what do you sell in here?" "Oh, just about anything!" "Anything?" "Yeah, anything you want. What do you want?" She said, "I don't know." "Well," Jesus said, "feel free, walk up and down the aisles, make a list, see what it is you want, and then come back and we'll see what we can do for you."

She did just that, walked up and down the aisles. There was peace on earth, no more war, no hunger or poverty, peace in families, no more drugs, harmony, clean air, careful use of resources. She wrote furiously. By the time she got back to the counter, she had a long list. Jesus took the list, skimmed through it, looked up at her and smiled. "No problem." And then he bent down behind the counter and picked out all sorts of things, stood up, and laid out the packets. She asked, "What are these?" Jesus replied, "Seed packets. This is a catalog store." She said, "You mean I don't get the finished product?" "No, this is a place of dreams. You come and see what it looks like, and I give you the seeds. You plant the seeds. You go home and nurture them and help them to grow and someone else reaps the benefits." "Oh," she said. And she left the store without buying anything.

If we don't get what we want right away, then maybe we don't really want it, or we don't want it enough. This is discouraging. We may have seen the dream of the kingdom. We may know exactly how the kingdom comes, but that doesn't mean that we bring it, or contribute to it, or are a part of it. We are all reaping the benefits of those who have gone before us in faith and life. But we need to stop and ask ourselves what we are doing for others. What seeds are we planting and nourishing? Our religion teaches that it is not primarily what we do for ourselves or our own, but what we do for others, for the outsiders, the strangers, that reveals our belief.

■ There was once an old Jewish man. All he ever did in his spare time was go to the edge of the village and plant fig trees. People would ask him, "Why are you planting fig trees? You are going to die before you can eat any of the fruit that they produce." But he said, "I have spent so many happy hours sitting under fig trees and eating their fruit. Those trees were planted by others. Why shouldn't I make sure that others will know the enjoyment that I have had?"

Our religion is the seeds that have been planted in us, that have been nurtured by many other people. Hopefully others will reap the benefits of what we begin and pass on. If we don't pass it on, it dies with us. The dream dies. A piece of the kingdom dies. There is no possibility if we don't plant. God relies on us to bring the kingdom. If it doesn't come on the earth, it is because most of us can't be bothered. We want it but not enough. It's too hard.

It is true that we can do very little alone; the kingdom comes in community. Leon Bloy says that he will know when he gets to the kingdom of heaven because the first thing God is going to say to him while he looks around is, "Where are all the others?"

The vision, the dream of the kingdom, is given to us in glimpses. Each time we get a glimpse it is as though we find the treasure hidden in the field. The moment we see that treasure we rejoice exceedingly, but then we must begin the work, the never-ending work. But we work together, not alone, and we have the privileges of the intimacy and support—and the hope.

3

The Sower and the Seed

———— ■ ————

■ *That same day Jesus left the house and sat down by the lakeside. As many people gathered in front and around him, he got in a boat. There he sat while the whole crowd stood on the shore, and spoke to them in parables about many things.*

Jesus said, "The sower went out to sow and some seeds fell along the path and the birds came and ate them up. Other seeds fell on rocky ground where there was little soil, and the seeds sprouted quickly because the soil was not deep. When the sun rose the plants were scorched and withered because they had no roots. Again other seeds fell among thistles; and the thistles grew and choked the plants. Still other seeds fell on good soil and produced a crop; some produced a hundredfold, others sixty and others thirty. If you have ears, then hear!" (Matthew 13:1-9).

Now in this parable there are four choices for the seed: seed that lands on a footpath, seed that falls on rocky ground, seed that falls among thorns and seed that falls in good ground and yields grain a hundred- or sixty- or thirtyfold. We'll start with what kind of seed we think ourselves to be. We often focus more on the images of the soil the seeds fall into than the kind of seeds they might be. All parables are dense with information, encoded, and we can start with just about any detail or image and look deeply into its meaning.

31

But we must choose an image. We can't say, I'm both, or sometimes this and that. We have to start somewhere.

What if we see ourselves as seed yielding a hundred- or sixty- or thirtyfold? What is it like to produce this yield? What would it be like to have a hundredfold yield every time we heard the word of God?—or even ninety or sixty or thirty? Even having children is having a yield, not seen so much as numbers but in terms of what kind of children they are becoming or have become in our family's field. We sow the seed in our children, our youth, our catechumens, and all we can do is stand in awe of God and know that it is God who has truly given the yield; God did this marvelous thing, and not us.

What makes seed grow? Do we make ourselves grow? Or is it God who gives growth and increase in our lives and churches? Usually we harvest what someone else has sowed. Yielding can also be frightening because it leads to the harvest. The whole reason for the sowing is the yield, the harvest, the cutting down of the crop to collect the grain to make wheat for bread, food for others to eat. This is, of course, connected to the words in John that "unless the seed falls into the ground and dies nothing comes forth." We sow to yield bread for others in the kingdom. The yield is for others, a responsibility we embrace.

Few of us see ourselves in the group that yields. Is that because we are humble? This virtue of humility, though, is not one of the strong virtues practiced in our church today. Being humble means being close to the ground, it means having a tendency to disappear without being remembered because what you did, you did anonymously. And when you have done much, everyone thinks someone else did it, and you can rejoice exceedingly in that fact.

Why do we choose one of the other places? Many choose the soil on the footpath, the edge. They see themselves as edge-walkers, having religion or an association with religion but skirting the real issues, being on the edge of the institution, parish, family, not wanting to get caught inside. The second place is the rocky ground, the shallow soil with an immediate response that quickly dies away. People see themselves as growing in fast spurts but then losing interest and intent just as quickly. They get scorched a lot and burned. Others fall among thorns, brush, thistles—they see that the company they keep is choking them to death. So much in the world mitigates against us and chokes the life of wonder or faith.

The sower, the farmer, went out sowing, broadside, and the seed lands everywhere, on footpaths, edges, among thorns, on hard ground and in good soil too. I once discussed this parable with a deaf community, and the people mimed it. One of the women was the sower, and as she flung her arms wide in a dance and moved around the room, the others would run and fall wherever they landed—into desks, the trash can, along the edges of the walls, in clumps together. The image was striking. It was very apparent that the seed is us, and that life is a field, and that we're all involved in it to one degree or another.

Some of us believe it's a question of luck. After all, it's the sower who throws the seed. It's not our fault that we land on the hard ground, among the rocks or thistles. And what image are we pursuing? Are we the ground or the seed? What is this seed that Jesus is sowing? What kind of ground are we? When the word of the Lord is sown—and Jesus is sowing broadside everywhere he goes, by the side of the lake with the crowds standing around listening to him—what kind of response, what kind of ground are we? Whom do we live with? What's around us? Whom do we hang around with? And remember, we know we're in good soil if we have a yield. But what are we yielding?

This story makes us uncomfortable. It forces us to decide where we are now, if we want to change, and what is entailed in that change or shift of place, shift of home-base? All of the parables, all of scripture is about us, telling us the truth about ourselves whether we want to deal with it or not. It asks us point blank what we are going to do with what we see in ourselves. And this conversion, this change has to be looked at not singularly but collectively, because we are in this field together. It is a field of family, parish, religious community, national boundaries, universal church, privileged interest groups, and so on. This field is watched by others for growth, increase and yield. It is obvious to others whether or not we are what we claim to be as believers in Jesus, as Christians and disciples living in community.

After our initial reaction, let us read the scripture again, along with Jesus' explanation further on in this chapter of Matthew, with an invocation to the Spirit to stir inside each of us in the hearing and call us to account for what kind of soil we have been in our lives.

■ *That same day Jesus left the house and sat down by the lakeside. As many people gathered in front and around him, he got in a boat. There he sat while the whole crowd stood on the shore, and spoke to them in parables about many things.*

Jesus said, "The sower went out to sow and some seeds fell along the path and the birds came and ate them up. Other seeds fell on rocky ground where there was little soil, and the seeds sprouted quickly because the soil was not deep. When the sun rose the plants were scorched and withered because they had no roots. Again other seeds fell among thistles; and the thistles grew and choked the plants. Still other seeds fell on good soil and produced a crop; some produced a hundredfold, others sixty and others thirty. If you have ears, then hear!"

Then his disciples came to him with the question, "Why do you speak to them in parables?"

Jesus answered, "To you it is given to know the secrets of the kingdom of Heaven, but not to these people. For they who have will be given more and they will have an abundance. But they who do not have will be deprived of even what they have. That is why I speak to them in parables, because they look and yet do not see; they hear, but they do not listen or understand.

In them the words of the prophet Isaiah come true: Much as you hear, you do not understand; much as you see, you do not perceive.

For the heart of this people has grown dull. Their ears hardly hear and their eyes dare not see. If they were to see with their eyes, hear with their ears and understand with their heart, they would turn back and I would heal them.

But blessed are your eyes because they see and your ears, because they hear.

For I tell you that many prophets and upright people would have liked to see the things you see, but they did not, and to hear the things you hear, but they did not hear it" (Matthew 13:1-17).

The reasoning behind this tactic of telling stories, of teaching in parables, is to make the people look and hear and realize that they are *not* looking, hearing and understanding. They are refusing consciously to respond and not allowing Jesus to heal them, convert them and tell them the truth. Jesus resorts to parables because our hearts are so sluggish, slow to respond and to take responsibility for who we are and what we do, religiously, humanly, with God and with one another.

But the kingdom is here with Jesus' presence as he comes among us, and it is a time of blessing, a time of beatitude and rejoicing. The time of the ancient prophecies is coming, the time is fulfilled, the long wait is ending, the moment that the prophets and holy ones, the saints, those who belong to God alone foresaw. God's kingdom is here now, and we get to see and hear and understand. This is one of the many beatitudes of Matthew's gospel. It is the blessing of open hearts and minds, open ears receptive to the Spirit and the truth, responsive to the kingdom and the proclamation of good news, the word of the Lord in Jesus' mouth. The style of the parable is prophetic, demanding reflection and response, conversion and humility, and acknowledgment that much is given and much is to be shared, that our lives belong to the kingdom and so, in God, to others. After telling the parable, Jesus continues, being more specific about the meaning of the ground and what happens when the word of the Lord falls into these different places and hearts. It is generally agreed that these parabolic explanations are later attempts of the early church communities to explain the parables, which were often difficult to understand.

■ *"Now listen to the parable of the sower.*

When people hear the message of the Kingdom, but fail to commit themselves to it, the devil comes and snatches away what was sown in their hearts. This is the seed that fell along the footpath.

The seed that fell on rocky ground stands for those who hear the word and accept it at once with joy. But it has no roots in them and lasts only for a short time. When they are harassed or persecuted because of the word, they soon give up.

The seed that fell among the thistles is the one who hears the word, but then the worries of this life and the empty promises of wealth choke the word, and it does not bear fruit.

But the seed that fell on good soil is the one who hears the word and understands it; this person bears fruit and produces a hundred, or sixty, or thirty times more" (Matthew 13:18-23).

The categories become a bit more specific within the context of church, especially Matthew's community of house church at the end of the first century, after the fall of Jerusalem. For Matthew the reactions are more pointed and personal. One of the important and hard things to learn to do with the parables is to not take them personally, but learn to take them to heart.

The second reading and reflection can bring us hope. The gospel is good news: to the poor, to those who yield, to those who give way to the kingdom of God, the word of the Lord in our midst. It allows us to see and acknowledge that we are in the field instead of on the footpath, that we may have been choked in the past but are no longer, that we are aware that we do not understand as much as we thought we did.

The soil is getting richer and deeper. It gives us a sense of the importance of the company we keep and the people we commit ourselves to in church. And we always know that it's about us, right here and now. We can begin to let the parables question and judge us. Is the story coming true *in* us, or is the story coming true *without* us? However, each story always offers a way out of any predicament in which we might find ourselves. Each story encourages us because it makes us feel that God is aware of us, careful of us and giving the grace and the increase and yield. We are to let it happen, and like Mary, God will do great things for us. God takes great delight in us, in our yield and in our harvest.

But the word also makes us responsible together. The seed is planted to bring forth the bread of life, bread for the world, the bread of justice and truth, of hope, Eucharist, the bread of peace, all shared, even shared possibilities. One grain of wheat doesn't go far, but a field of wheat feeds many.

The parable is also worrisome. Jesus is telling these things to his disciples and reminding them to remember that they don't understand it all yet and perhaps they never will understand completely. After all, how long have we been listening to the word of the Lord and what have we really understood or put into practice? Why are we only yielding 30 percent? After all, if we have an investment, what kind of yield do we want to see coming back? If we anticipate only 2 or 3 percent we're not overjoyed with the investment. What if God feels the same way about all that is invested in us, in the church, in his disciples? What has been sowed in us? Is it coming out, yielding in great heart, great generosity, great justice and compassion? Is it expanding? Are our families, our parishes, our dioceses yielding? When others look at us, what do they see? A lot of folk on the footpaths, a lot among thorns, a lot who are very shallow? Or do they see a field that is ready to harvest?

This seed that is the word of God is also the treasure hidden in the field. It is also the relationship we have with God and one another in the field. Once we own the field, it is time to sow, to buy the best seed and sow broadside, liberally, everywhere. We become the sower with the word of God, the treasure, the relationship that we want to scatter everywhere in the world so that others might know rejoicing, so that they may find and come to join us in the venture of selling all and staking our lives on that field and treasure and hope.

Now let's talk about the yield of the field. This is the heart of the parable, its devastating call to recognize and assess our lives in response to the word that is preached among us. What is a typical yield for a crop sowed at the time of Jesus? What would the hearers expect as a good yield? After all, they plowed the field, sowed, prayed and hoped for rain, good weather, good seed. Even though they worked hard, there was no guarantee of a harvest, especially in a climate as arid and barren as that of Palestine. So many factors could affect the yield even without the threats of war, drought, oppression, forced labor or higher taxes on the yield.

What is a good yield from good seed (the word of God)? A good yield on a field in Jesus' Palestine—sowed broadside, with basic plowing, given a dry area, wind, sun, heat, lack of rain, along with an occupied territory, and so on—was between 2 to 8 percent. Such a yield on all the seed in a field would enable the farmer to more than break even for the year. In fact the farmer could afford to buy the best seed available for the following year, fix up the barn and come up with extras—food, clothing, equipment. With 15 percent yield the farmer could pay off debts, get out from under. With 20 or 25 percent? Perhaps buy a neighbor's fields, put in irrigation ditches, put up a new barn. 30 to 60 percent? Maybe have a monopoly on the product in the state and control that market. And 90 percent? This is an international, transnational corporation controlling not only the market but politics and trade, communications and nations as well. 100 percent? The farmer owns it all.

This is a parable about farming, sowing and harvesting; about economics, politics, human commerce; about ordinary experiences of life among people. Many of those listening to Jesus were farmers, sharecroppers working on others' lands. They hear this story about a farmer sowing good seed and the land, the field that receives it, and they wonder about the harvest, the crop. But the seed is the word of God, the treasure hidden in the field, which plants the longing and the loving of justice, mercy, peace and reconciliation in people in a community.

If the word of God gets a twofold yield in our hearts, in our parish or diocese, what is happening? Everyone is involved, everyone in our immediate environs is taken care of and included. The harvest is great, the justice and peace tangible. With a fifteenfold yield in a parish or diocese, what is noticeable? The early church was described in the Didache, a second-century document, with the words, "See how those Christians love one another, there are no poor among them." Love was apparent, vibrantly, wondrously so! So, there would be no poor in our parishes and neighborhoods and, of course, people would be flocking to church for help, solace, companionship, hope and community. It would be clear to all, both those in church and not, that something was happening, growing and being produced here in this place.

If there was a yield of sixtyfold or more, Christians would be a force to be reckoned with in any country, a moral pressure, a majority, not necessarily in numbers but in influence. They could not be ignored. Their influence would be noticeable and strong in education, politics, economics, communication, laws, in all areas of human endeavor and values. A yield of ninety- or one hundredfold would show us the kingdom of heaven, because we would dwell in it even now, especially if this were the experience of the universal church. But, of course, long before that, the members of the church, the communities, the field, would be persecuted and hounded, feared and respected because of their belief, their faithfulness. Their religious practice would seep through all their behavior, relationships and institutions.

The reality, of course, is very different. The parable gives us hope that on some levels, personally perhaps, and here and there as church, we are doing something. However, generally speaking, on larger issues and scope there isn't much of a yield. Others, especially those who can be more objective about the issue, those who are outside the field, look at us and don't see a group of people or individuals who are much different from themselves.

A couple of years ago the *New York Times* surveyed American Catholics and American non-Catholics on where they stood on the major moral issues of abortion, the death penalty, euthanasia, the build-up and use of nuclear weapons and arms treaties, fair trade agreements that gave the United States an advantage, and the use of economic budgets and subsidies for basic human resources in the area of health, education, welfare, housing, job training, and so on. What they found was revealing and, to anyone who thinks about it, disheartening and discouraging. There were about 45 to 55 million Catholics in a population of 245 to 255 million Americans, and the statistical difference was less than half a percent. The yield was near nonexistent.

And yet the word of the Lord is so powerful and potent, the seed so strong and good, that out of practically nothing, goodness, mercy, justice and peace can grow! What does God want of us, our parishes, dioceses, universal church? What is expected from the seed, the word of God, the presence of the Lord in our midst? One of the most hopeful parts of this parable is to note that there is a new crop, a new time to sow every year. Every year we start again. Every year the seed is sown again in our hearts.

Our whole liturgical celebration and practice is based on the sowing of the word, which is timeless, potent, evocative and powerful. We ritualize and incorporate in our own bodies and communities the Spirit who makes the word incarnate, who brings the seed to fruition, who heals and helps us to bear in our bodies the presence of the Lord in the earth. By resurrection we are even told that the earth itself is sown with this newness and vibrancy and that all of creation is groaning for completion, for fullness, for the kingdom to come in its full glory and strength in history and in our world.

The Word took flesh in Mary, was born in Jesus and is shared with us in baptism, Eucharist and confirmation. We are called to yield and bear fruit to whatever capacity we can: thirty-, or sixty- or ninetyfold. And if we only have a year—that is, in the sense that each liturgical year begins with Advent—then what will this year yield? Do I want a yield of sixtyfold in my life or our parish this year? Then what are we going to do personally and collectively to make sure that the yield is given? What do we have to do this year? What does this do to us or mean for our lives now? This question is the logical end of the parable. This is what it is meant to change in us, for even at this moment the sower is planting the seed, throwing it out again among us, and waiting to see what kind of ground it falls on in our hearts.

As Jesus says, we are sluggish, our hearts are stubborn, and we firmly close our eyes, but the moment the parable breaks through the veils and the vision opens up, we are caught in its light and questioned. And in that moment there is the possibility, the grace that we will see and hear and understand with our hearts and turn back and be healed. The parable challenges us and reminds us how long we have been baptized, how long we have been with Jesus, how long we have been in this field, how long we have been hearing the scriptures and studying them and praying over them, even preparing sermons on them. What is the seed yielding in us?

We must begin today, as though the seed is just now sown. Just because there was a good crop this past year doesn't mean that it necessarily will happen again. The parable makes us attentive to history today, to here and now, to the invitation and the Spirit who is trying to invade our lives. It can fire us with enthusiasm, with hope, since this word is so powerful.

Hope is a virtue that is not necessarily based on reality. Hope is based, along with all the other virtues, on grace. What can God do with us? What are the outrageous, limitless expectations God has of us, expectations that we don't really believe or trust? Hope is the key to believing in the passion of possibility. Jesus has entrusted this dream, this hope to us and told us to do something with it. We're not to keep it or hoard it. The whole structure and liturgy of the church is set up so that hope keeps returning, coming back, and we have marvelous opportunities to act on the word and start over again. The day of the sun, Sunday, tells us each time we gather as believers we can begin again, that resurrection is in our midst and that every sunrise we are nudged into belief, into living in hope and surviving with gracefulness.

Jesus will say over and over again in his encounters with sinners and his disciples, "Today salvation has come to this house," and the psalmist sings out, "This is the day that the Lord has made, let us be glad and rejoice in it." Today is this day, every day, any day. Today we can start. Today everything can start. There is only today with God, because of grace, the Spirit and forgiveness given in the hope of our belief.

Each moment the seed is being sown. But we must remember the process—God sows the seed, we do some work, and someone else reaps the benefit. That is the pattern, age-old and repetitive and productive. We ourselves are products of that ritual. All that we have is the result of reaping the benefits of someone else's hard work, belief and endurance. This attitude is part of the sowing of the seed, the hearing of the gospel and the yield.

This is an awareness of how community operates and works very specifically and enduringly. This field, this church, this community is the Body of Christ, is Eucharist, is the harvest, the yield, and we are becoming the seed for bread for the world together. Our liturgies reflect the quality of life in our communities for better or worse, in season and out.

We go home to the fullness of this field, this kingdom of heaven, with others. It's nearly impossible to go home alone. We are known here by the company we keep, those we break bread with, the stories we tell. One day in the fullness of hope we will still be known by that company, those who went off and dwelled in the company of Jesus as his disciples, his friends.

This brings up the thought: What if we are going to get into the kingdom of heaven only if everybody else in our parish or religious community does? This is a sobering thought, and one that follows easily from this sense of the field, the yield. The yield is communal. The harvest is together. There are only two choices: wheat or weeds, which, of course, is the next parable. We have to start thinking together as the Body of Christ, connected, united in the power of the Spirit and becoming community, in communion with the word of God, becoming wheat that can be ground into flour and made into bread for the feeding of the world. Are we becoming the bread of hope, the bread of justice, sustaining the world and luring others into the field, the kingdom of heaven? This parable gives hope and sobers us, making us look at how we journey home to the fullness of this kingdom of peace and justice.

If this seed has been sown in us for years, then sooner or later we must become the sower and go out into the world, the other fields, and sow there what has been sown in us. After the resurrection Jesus' first words to his disciples when he breaks into their locked room is, "Peace be with you. As the Father has sent me, so now I send you." We are the adult children of God, called to become not just seed for the bread, but seed for the sowing and the sower. This is the job, the mission and vocation that has been entrusted to all of us by the resurrection. This seed sown in us, in baptism and in every moment since in the community, is pure gift given.

The Native Americans have a saying that a gift is not a gift until it is given twice, at least twice. And that speaks of what God has given to us, sowing broadside, generously, in the word, the scriptures, the understanding of the hearts of the community and especially in its taking root in our lives and history. Our faith is not a gift until it has been given at least twice.

There is a story that brings home this parable of the seed sown in the field. It is a Sufi teaching story from the Muslim tradition.

■ Once upon a time there was a raven, just an ordinary black bird. He used to love to fly off early in the morning and find a perch and stay for the day and watch the world happen. Then at night he'd head back to the rookery and share all his tales and experiences of what he saw that day. Well, one day he found a perch in a high old tree and settled down for the day. And he didn't have long to wait. Soon, a hunter approached and stopped right underneath his tree. The hunter set to work diligently, first positioning small traps, dozens of them, all around the base of the tree. Then he set the snares so that the slightest movement would trigger the snare and catch whatever touched it. Then he scattered seed liberally and thickly under the tree. Lastly he hung a huge net, hidden in the branches of the tree, and stepped back to look at his handiwork. He was pleased and slipped off further into the forest to wait and see what he could catch.

The raven had watched fascinated and he waited, too, to see what would happen. He didn't have long to wait. Soon, high above him, a flock of pigeons flew over. They stopped almost in mid-air, seeing all the seed and grain scattered down below under the tree and, of course, not seeing the snares and the great net hanging and waiting as well.

They circled, getting ready to swoop down. At the very last minute, the raven cried out loudly, "Caw, caw! Don't, brothers and sisters. It's a trap." There was great squawking and a flurry of wings as the pigeons regrouped and finally the leader called back, "Oh, it's a trap all right, but you are the one who thinks to set it. You want all that seed for yourself. Well, we aren't that easily taken in!"

And with that the pigeons swooped down, landed under the tree, right under the raven and began to eat. But with every step, they triggered a snare, one after another, as they greedily ate and then without warning, the net fell and caught them all. There was a terrible squawking and loud flapping of wings, but no matter how hard they tried, they couldn't move the heavy net.

Finally, the pigeon cried out to the raven, "We're sorry, you were right. Can you help us get free?" The raven couldn't believe how stupid the pigeons were, but he had compassion on them and said, "Yes, but you must do exactly what I say. First, shut up." Now this was very hard for the pigeons, because now they could hear the hunter coming through the forest and they knew their death was imminent. "Second, do exactly what I tell you. At the count of three, all of you rise together. Then, when you lift the net, follow me. I will take you to a field near here where I have some friends, the mice, and they will chew the net and you will be free."

They finally settled down, and just in time too. The raven cried out, "One, two, three, rise!" And all the pigeons rose as one. The last thing the hunter saw was a flock of pigeons carrying his net, following a raven away across the tree tops. They followed the raven and dropped down in the field. The mice appeared and chewed the net, setting the pigeons free. Again, there was a loud noise and flapping of wings.

Finally things settled down, and the leader approached the raven again. "How can we thank you for saving our lives?" The raven said, "You can't. But there are a few things you can learn from this experience. Listen very carefully. First, when you get yourself into something stupid, everybody shut up. Number two, decide who it is you are going to obey. Three, all of you rise together and bear your burden as one. And four, make friends with the mice in faraway fields. And lastly, when someone warns you about your greed, listen."

And with that the birds flew off, and the raven returned to his rookery that night with his story. And when they tell this story, they ask, "And who have you been acting like lately, the stupid pigeons or the raven?"

And so we dwell together in the field. Life in the field can be like that of the pigeons or the raven, and the field can be

fertile or barren. Jesus goes on to talk about his kingdom
and this field.

■ *Jesus told them another parable, "The kingdom of Heaven can
be compared to a sower who sowed good seed in the field. While
everyone was asleep, enemies came and sowed weeds among the
wheat, and left.*

*When the plants sprouted and produced grain, the weeds also
appeared. Then the servants came to the owner and said: 'Sir, it
was good seed that you sowed in your field; where did the weeds
come from?'*

*The owner answered them: 'This is the work of an enemy.'
They asked: 'Do you want us to go and pull up the weeds?' The
owner told them: 'No, when you pull up the weeds, you might
uproot the wheat with them. Let them just grow together until
harvest; then I will tell the workers: Pull up the weeds first, tie
them in bundles and burn them; then gather the wheat into my
barn" (Matthew 13:24-30).*

The parable seems to be cut and dried, ending rather
abruptly with the harvest, a simple straightforward description of a field, except for a catch—the weeds are planted by
an enemy. There are only two choices when we hear the parable: are we weeds or are we maturing into wheat? Others
can already see, at least those who are the slaves of the master and concerned with the field's harvest and yield.

This parable can almost be read as an old-time movie with
villains and heroes, the bad and the good sides. Again,
mimed by a deaf community it can be hilarious. First the
good seed gets sowed, with bodies falling over happily and
grouping themselves somewhat together in a field. Then
night falls and the enemy, complete with great moustache,
comes stealthily and sinisterly sows bad seed, and goes away
laughing gleefully. Then the seed starts to mature. The good
seed slowly rises, happy as a lark, dancing in the field. Then
the weeds make their appearance. They come up wrapping
themselves around the wheat, choking, glaring, tickling and
generally being a nuisance and enjoying every moment. The
servants appear and approach their master, intent on rout-
ing out the weeds, fixing the field, sure of themselves and
their knowledge of the difference, sure that the weeds need

to be eliminated. They are cautioned to let them grow together, because in pulling out the weeds, which have very strong intertwining root systems, they will pull up the wheat as well. Wait.

The enemy's hand is seen for what it is. The enemy's presence is seen and acknowledged in the weeds, but there is to be no violent war or struggle in the field. They will grow together until the harvest, until the maturation process is finished and the growing cycle is complete. Then, at harvest, the master sends his harvesters into the field and the weeds are collected and the wheat is gathered. There are only two ends: bundling to burn or being gathered into the barn. Where is the barn? Does living in the field lead to living in the barn or is the barn just a temporary place? Does the real parable begin with remembering what wheat is planted for, for the making of bread, for the feeding of the earth and the children of earth? This wheat, this bread, is the substance of life.

How exactly does one grow? Parables are about everyday occurrences: how does any seed grow? Seeds grow with sun, water, time, sometimes cultivation, but seeds also can grow without attention. Certainly weeds seem to do just fine on their own. What is sun, water, time, cultivation for wheat, for those in the field becoming bread for the world? The sun of justice, the waters of baptism, the times of the year, ordinary and extraordinary times of liturgy, the hearing and the practice of the scriptures, the discipline of community, the corporal and spiritual works of mercy, the tendering of hope, of forgiveness and reconciliation. We have lots of practice with the weeds all around us, sharing the same ground, the same sun, water, time and cultivation.

And who are the servants, the slaves of the master, the owner? Are we the wheat/weeds or are we the slaves? Do we belong to someone? To whom do we belong? To whom is our allegiance? Parables, like all stories, but perhaps even more so, are layered. If we are weeds and wheat we ask one set of questions, relating to how we live in the field with others of like mind and others who cause difficulty in our living conditions. If we are slaves of the owner in the story, there will be other questions regarding our responsibilities toward others in our care and charge and how we are to act in relation to obstacles and problems. Both sets of questions will deal with violence and nonviolence, aggressive reactions and judgments and how to dwell in peace so that others may just have a chance to live and grow, to mature and come to their promised fulfillment.

■ Frog was in his garden. Toad came walking by. "What a fine garden you have, Frog," he said. "Yes," said Frog. "It is very nice, but it was hard work." "I wish I had a garden," said Toad. "Here are some flower seeds. Plant them in the ground," said Frog, "and soon you will have a garden." "How soon?" asked Toad. "Quite soon," said Frog. Toad ran home. He planted the flower seeds. "Now seeds," said Toad, "start growing." Toad walked up and down a few times. The seeds did not start to grow. Toad put his head close to the ground and said loudly, "Now seeds, start growing!" Toad looked at the ground again. The seeds did not start to grow. Toad put his head very close to the ground and shouted, "NOW SEEDS, START GROWING!" Frog came running up the path. "What is all this noise?" he asked. "My seeds will not grow," said Toad. "You are shouting too much," said Frog. "These poor seeds are afraid to grow." "My seeds are afraid to grow?" asked Toad. "Of course," said Frog. "Leave them alone for a few days. Let the sun shine on them, let the rain fall on them. Soon your seeds will start to grow." That night Toad looked out of his window. "Drat!" said Toad. "My seeds have not started to grow. They must be afraid of the dark." Toad went out to his garden with some candles. "I will read a story," said Toad. "Then they will not be afraid." Toad read a long story to his seeds. All the next day Toad sang songs to his seeds. And all the next day Toad read poems to his seeds. And all the next day Toad played music for his seeds. Toad looked at the ground. The seeds still did not start to grow. "What shall I do?" cried Toad. "These must be the most frightened seeds in the whole world!" Then Toad felt very tired, and he fell asleep. "Toad, Toad, wake up," said Frog. "Look at your garden!" Toad looked at his garden. Little green plants were coming up out of the ground. "At last," shouted Toad, "my seeds have stopped being afraid to grow!" "And now you will have a nice garden too," said Frog. "Yes," said Toad, "but you were right, Frog. It was very hard work."[1]

Most of the time we are like Toad, thinking that what we do makes the seeds grow, forgetting that a great deal more is at work than just us and our small endeavors or contributions to the project. Time is of the essence, and time proves much in maturation, in growth, in change and transformation. After all, when confronted with any sort of judgment, of choice, decision or outcome, most of us just want a little more time. Here the parable is hopeful. There is time. We all grow together until the harvest. The trick is knowing when the harvest time approaches.

Liturgically, each year the church looks at the end of time, the end of the year, the end of things as they are and looks to inclusion and exclusion, to whether or not we are within the kingdom's confines and boundaries or whether we are out. The last Sundays of the year, in mid-fall, late November, when all is harvested and winter has set in in the northern hemisphere, is the time for reflection, for a hard look at whether we are weeds or wheat at this moment and if the end were now, would we be bundled and burned or gathered into the barn for threshing and being made into flour for bread.

Later on, the disciples come to Jesus and ask him to explain the parable. This is generally agreed to be a later addition to the text, from the early church's interpretation and expectation of the more immediate end times or coming of the kingdom in fullness, which of course didn't come and hasn't come yet. The explanation reads:

> Then he sent the crowds away and went into the house. And his disciples came to him saying, "Explain to us the parable of the weeds in the field." Jesus answered them, "The one who sows the good seed is the Son of Man. The field is the world; the good seed are the people of the Kingdom; the weeds are those who belong to the

---

[1]   Arnold Lobel, "The Garden," *Frog and Toad Together* (New York: Harper & Row, 1971), pp. 18-30.

evil one. The enemy who sows them is the devil; the harvest is the end of time and the workers are the angels.

Just as the weeds are pulled up and burned in the fire, so will it be at the end of time. The Son of Man will send his angels, and they will weed out of his kingdom all that is scandalous and all who do evil. And these will be thrown in the blazing furnace, where there will be weeping and gnashing of teeth. Then the just will shine like the sun in the kingdom of their Father. If you have ears, then hear" (Matthew 13:36-43).

It is blunt, to the point, and it turns the parable into an allegory. An allegory explains a story or a set of images and symbols by saying this is to this as this is to that. It is an explanation, a description of a set reality, whereas the parable is much more open-ended. This interpretation is one of many, one that was used because people were expecting the end-times, a time of judgment that was close and universal in history. But judgment comes yearly as we gather together in the barns and begin again with the old stories, to open them up and plant them again in the history of the world that is packed with weeds and wheat, in churches and communities that are intertwined as weeds and wheat. Like the slaves in the story, we want action now, usually violent action that separates the weeds and wheat here and now, and that would leave some of us in very hot water.

There is a short story that is told among the Sufi, a teaching story that can be used when looking at any of the parables. It convicts us, challenges us and calls us to account, rather than letting us use the parable on the outside world, or others in our community or families.

■ Sufi Jalaluddin Rumi was a remarkable teacher, poet, dancer and prayer, and one day a newly arrived searcher came and approached him asking: "Master, are you ready to teach me?" The master looked the searcher steadily in the eyes and searching into them asked: "That depends: are you ready to learn from me?"

There is an urgency in this story. It too is a parable, and it conveys the bluntness and the intensity of the questioning of the parable form. Are we ready? Are we so sure we are either the wheat or the slaves of the master? How much resistance resides in us to the truth, to being seen as weeds or those who serve the enemy? What would it take for us to acknowledge that we are the weeds, that we are choking and threatening the growth of others in our selfish disregard, intent on our own space? What would it take for us to be stopped in our tracks, to be rebuked and obey the commands of a nonviolent way of life and time in regards to all those we see as difficult or problematic? What would it take for us to be caught up short and acknowledge that we serve our own ends and so serve the enemy instead of serving God? What would it take for us to be seen as self-righteous, destructive in our judgments and behavior toward others? Any pat answers basically destroy the layers of the parable, which is told to confront us, convict us, challenge us to change.

The next parable follows the interpretation of the treasure and the field and the pearl of great price. It echoes this same theme with a new twist:

■ *"Again, the kingdom of Heaven is like a big fishing net let down into the sea, where every kind of fish has been caught. When the net is full, it is dragged ashore. Then they sit down and gather the good fish in buckets, but throw the worthless ones away. That is how it will be at the end of time; the angels will go out to separate the wicked from the just and throw them into the blazing furnace, where they will weep and gnash their teeth."*

Jesus asked, "Have you understood all these things?" "Yes," they answered. So he said to them, "You will see that every teacher of the Law who becomes a disciple of the Kingdom is like a householder who can produce from the store of things both old and new."

When Jesus had finished these parables, he left the place (Matthew 13:47-53).

"Have you understood all these things?" And the disciples, Jesus' listeners, glibly say without qualms, "Yes." Ludicrous, as though mystery can be so easily understood, incorporated and made into flesh and blood in our lives after one or two hearings. And Jesus encourages his listeners to become learned in the kingdom, the reign of God, like the head of a household who knows everything that is in the storeroom.

Learned in the kingdom, the reign of God: what does that entail? The image evokes family, ties, responsibilities and privileges shared among those with power and those who serve the master, who is owner of the field. It is an issue of crossing lines, borders, and nationalities and differences to share in the blood ties of community and church as disciples and companions of the risen Lord among us, hidden in the least of our brothers and sisters.

The word *reign* can be broadened. *Reign* has historical echoes of government, nations ruled by kings, knights and ladies, peasants, warring countries and a hierarchy that deals in laws, relations and economics, hereditary and serf rights, and so on. But the word *reign* is also related to the word *rein*: a discipline, a hold, a check that controls, a way of being in life. These reins stop, slow down, give direction to and alter paths. The rein of God, heaven's rein, operates like reins on the world, on evil, on circumstances and on people, especially those who freely accept the rein as part of belonging to one another.

And the word *reign* recalls *rain*, the rain that falls from the sky, as described in Isaiah like the word of the Lord that comes like rain and snow, that waters the earth and does not return to heaven, to God, until it does what it was told to do. In the Native American communities, especially in the southwest, there are two kinds of rain: male and female rain, each serving a different function and coming at different times. Male rain comes hard, driving and fast. It is often short-lived, but it comes most often in spring and is enough to push the seed into the ground and get it started in the germination process. Female rain comes later in the summer months when the crops are up and high and the heat is thick. It comes softly, gently, and hangs in the sky, often evaporating before it touches the ground. But it cools the air and moistens the crops and eases the day, allowing the crops to continue growing, their thirst slaked. The kingdom of heaven is like rain, sometimes male and sometimes female, always nurturing, deepening, adding life.

So this reign of God, this kingdom of heaven, is rich, not just in allusion and symbol but in reality and in concrete expressions in the world of believers and those who practice this rein, this rain, this reign of relations, this place of justice and peace and hope, this position of service, as slaves and servants, this reality of God present in the world now. Parables operate like the kingdom itself. This story form gives us an experience of the kingdom. The form itself operates as the kingdom does. It creeps up on us, again and again, sometimes subtly and sometimes like a sledge hammer and then again like a soft shower falling upon us. The form of the parable subverts reality and undermines existing structures and relationships and attitudes, just as the kingdom does, whether we are aware of it or not, in it or not, converted by it or not. The parable form is like a current, drawing us deeper and deeper.

Jesus only teaches in parables after a certain point. This form assumes that the hearer has an open mind and heart, is receptive to being confronted and converted, is ready to learn about the kingdom, is vulnerable enough to say, "Maybe I'm wrong, maybe I don't know, maybe the things I'm most sure of are a bit off, especially in the areas of justice, God, community, mercy, sin and spirit. Maybe I've been teaching the wrong stuff, maybe my alliances are in the wrong places and my motives aren't all they seem to be."

The parable form reveals the teller's frustration: frustration at those hearing who will not make choices, who will not change, who only want to hear, discuss and stay in their own pockets of reality and not change, certainly not undermine all they have worked so hard to establish. The parable form says that we have to decide about the kingdom, and we have to decide now. Do we want into this relationship with God and others and earth or not? No more discussion—choose and do something. How many chances do we get? The parable form is a very confrontational form, just as the kingdom is. It is subversive, coming up and in from underneath, the way the kingdom comes, from underneath, from below, in incarnation and the poor, the least of the community. It is like quicksand, sucking us in. It looks just like all the other sand and ground, but the minute we step onto it, we begin to sink, we know we are in deep and going in over our head. It is a dangerous form, and we have an experience of these new relationships and how they turn the world and our life upside down. The more we listen, the deeper and more penetrating the experience becomes, the more a decision is required, demanded. There is no escape.

All the parables are about ordinary reality, but all of a sudden reality is not operating according to the usual rules—thank God—all is up for grabs, usually upside down. The parables deal most often with the issues of how the kingdom comes in the presence of violence and opposition, in relation to money, greed, selfishness and economics, politics, racism and social biases and classes, both personal and communal.

In this chapter the locus of the kingdom is a field of weeds and wheat and a net that drags up anything in the lake. It sets us up with an ordinary event and then throws in hints that something else is operating. At the end of the story we find we are sitting on the floor, with the rug pulled out from underneath us, and we're not too sure how we got there. First, this is our life, the way we expect it to be, and then it isn't at all. Something happens to us in the telling of the story—if we have the ears to hear. The story begins when the teller stops talking, when the tale is told, when the parable stops for breath, in that pause . . . and knowing look. The story uses our life experience and what we are attached to in order to do us in. Every time we hear the word of the Lord, the story really begins when the words are done. That is when we decide if we are going to make it come true or not. Is our version of reality going to match up with Jesus' God, or are we going to cling to our previous versions and stand against this new story, this new vision, new structure and new sense of life and death? Will we stand and resist or become part of the new reality—there are only two choices.

All the parables are intent on questioning us about our commitments, our allegiances. They ask to whom we belong—in these parables to the field of wheat or to the dragnet as fish for food. There is a Jewish story that throws us a curve on this issue.

■ Once upon a time, two families came to a rabbi wanting him to settle a dispute about the boundaries of their land. He listened to the members of one family as they recounted how they had received this land as their inheritance from their ancestors and how it had been in their family for generations. They had maps and papers to prove it. Then the rabbi listened to the other family. Its members described how they had lived on the land for years, working it and harvesting it. They claimed that they knew the land intimately and that it was their land. They didn't have the papers to prove it, but they had the calluses and sore backs and the harvest and the produce of the land. The rabbi looked at them both and backed away from between them. They turned on him and said, "Decide, rabbi, who owns this land." But the rabbi knelt down on the land and put his ear to the ground, listening. Finally he stood up and looked at both families. He said: "I had to listen to both of you, but I had to listen to the land, the center of this dispute also, and the land has spoken. It has told me this: 'Neither of you owns the land you stand on. It is the land that owns you.' "

What is it that owns us? What is the relationship turned upside down? Does God own us? Or are we busy in our debates and quarrels with others, claiming that we own God and trying to make him serve us and our needs? The parables turn on us and turn us upside down. Does the kingdom, the field, the community own us as master, as lord? Whom do we serve? Do we serve the kingdom, the field, the net, the will of God, or are our priorities elsewhere? G. K. Chesterton described St. Francis as standing always on his head and seeing the world from that vantage point. And, of course, that is the way the world really is from God's point of view. The parables stand us on our heads so that the vantage point of God confronts us and doesn't let us escape easily into our assumptions and comfortable ways of viewing life and God.

Have we understood all this? Are we learned in the kingdom of God, the reign of justice? Are we the head of the household of God, knowing what to draw forth for others, both the old and the new? Are we weeds? Are we useless, to be thrown away in the end? When the angels come, which group will we find ourselves in?

The parables say that what's wrong with the world is wrong with us. What's wrong with the church is wrong with us. What's wrong with economics, politics and structures is wrong with us. Decide. Decide now. The parable form hits every sensitive nerve in us and scrapes along it, making us shudder and react. Then it is up to us to decide whether to hear the message and live with it or to reject it and resist this version of reality. We hear it where we live, in our hearts and relationships, our values and choices, and it hurts, hurts hard. Who is in the kingdom of heaven if we are not? What if they are the ones who decide if we get in or not? Who are the real slaves of the master, the harvesters and the fishermen, the angels? Are we in their company? And what must we do to be in this kingdom, to be in relation with this God, to be friends with this master and lord?

There is yet another parable in this chapter of Matthew.

■ *He proposed still another parable: "The reign of God is like a mustard seed, which someone took and sowed in his field. It is the smallest seed of all, yet when full-grown it is the largest of plants. It becomes so big a shrub that the birds of the sky come and build their nests in its branches" (Matthew 13:31-32).*

This image is old, also found in this modified form in the book of Ezekiel 17:22-24:

■ *Thus says the Lord Yahweh: "At the top of the cedar I will take one of its uppermost branches, a tender twig and plant it. On a lofty, massive mountain, on a high mountain of Israel I will plant it. It will produce branches and bear fruit and become a magnificent cedar. Birds of all kinds will nest in it and find shelter in its branches. And all the trees of the field shall know that I am Yahweh, I who bring down the lofty tree and make the lowly tree tall. I will make the tree that is full of sap wither and the dry tree bloom. I, Yahweh, have spoken and this will I do."*

These short stories are about sowing and what grows forth from something tiny and inconsequential. A seed that becomes a bush, a plant that expands out and is so large, secure and encompassing that the birds of heaven come and nest in its branches. If this kingdom, this reign, this place, this community of Jesus is a mustard plant—or a magnificent cedar—who is nesting in our branches, which birds come to dwell with us in safety, hidden from the outside world in a secure place where the young can be nurtured and grow up knowing a home? The birds of the sky come to build their nests, all kinds of birds, all sorts of folk, little ones, swallows, larks, ravens, pigeons, unnumbered.

Where I live there are great trees, and at dusk and dawn the birds nesting in one or two large trees or bushes sing and chatter. The noise level is deafening, but not a single creature can be seen. Is the kingdom here on earth like that? Are our churches and communities like that for the poor and the least of the world? Is the universal church this great sheltering tree of lost migratory birds? Whom do we hide and to whom do we give security in our lives?

And lastly Jesus offers still another image:

■ *"The reign of God is like yeast which a woman took and kneaded into three measures of flour. Eventually the whole mass of dough began to rise" (Matthew 13:33).*

That's it—like the yield in the field, the great mustard plant and a mass of dough. The kingdom starts out small, and if the conditions are right— heat and temperature and moisture—it spreads, expands, grows, takes on a life of its own, becoming larger than anything we might expect.

One thing all these images have in common is compassion, basic needs and hospitality: wheat for making flour, flour and yeast for making bread, branches for shelter and home, being fish or useful in the net, yielding and being harvested for the needs of others, daily needs. Is that the single-hearted and single-minded reason for our communities: caring for the basic needs of others, the flocks of others, the masses of others in the world, as God in Jesus cared for humanity in the incarnation, the small seed that grew up to be the sun of justice, the child of God, the Son of Man, the hope of the nations, the bread of compassion? This is the seed planted in us, the treasure hidden in the scriptures, the church, the community, our hearts, the field of grace, history, the world. This is the pearl of great price, the one really valuable pearl, the dragnet, the seed on good ground, the good seed in the field, the presence of God in our midst. And so Jesus begins in earnest to preach this kingdom, the reign, the relationship, this vision of reality, this version of justice, and he says solemnly: "I will speak in parables. I will proclaim things kept secret since the beginning of the world" (Matthew 13:35). Let everyone heed what he hears!

This chapter that begins with the seed parables and preaching of the kingdom of God ends with Jesus going to his native place. In the synagogue at Nazareth all the people are filled with amazement, but dubious because they know him as the carpenter's son, Mary's son, brother to James, Joseph, Simon and Judas. "And so they took offense at him," and Jesus leaves his own house, his own place, and did not work miracles because of their lack of faith (Matthew 13:54-58).

The parables are desperate attempts to grasp hold of peoples' hearts and shake them into a new position, to unsettle very settled ways and people, to overturn our pasts and certainty and to startle us into sight and vision. This telling of stories, this announcement of good news in parables and this pulling us into hope in the kingdom of heaven here and now is hard work. There is much resistance, especially if we think we know God and think we are already in the kingdom of heaven and that the reign of God is ours to administer because we know the rules and ways of God, because we have always known God and the way things are. This is the backdrop for the parables.

We end with a Japanese folk saying: The scent of the flowers remains on the hands of the person who gives the gift away. This is the way the kingdom comes, yielding the treasure to others, giving away the pearl of great price, making bread and opening our arms so that others can come and find a home secure in us.

4

The First and the Last

———— ■ ————

Our opening parable comes from the orthodox Jewish community of the late Middle Ages in what is now eastern Europe. Many of the stories from this age refer to heaven and portray St. Peter at the gates, holding the keys to the kingdom. The reason for this, of course, is that Jews lived in a dominantly Christian culture. As a result, they incorporated the daily beliefs and understandings of that culture into their own religious storytelling. This parable is called "The Rabbi at Heaven's Gates." Keep in mind that in the Jewish and Christian traditions the words *justice, holiness, righteousness,* and *loving kindness* are almost interchangeable in their meanings and descriptions of both God and the people of God who obey the law.

■ Once upon a time there was a very holy and wise rabbi who loved the Torah, the scriptures, passionately. His whole life revolved around the word, and he was recognized as a living torah because of his belief and his practice, which was generous, universal and single-minded. He had many disciples and students, and people from many distant countries came to him for advice and prayer. Many came to his study houses just to be in his presence for a short while and to be able to say that they had been his student, that they had known him face to face. For the people believed that if their rabbi was holy, then his holiness rubbed off on them and affected their life and soul.

And then one day he died and found himself at the gates of heaven. He was horrified to find that Peter was standing at the gates, and he thought to himself: Did I miss the Messiah? Has my life been all in vain? And yet, to his surprise, Peter threw open the gates of heaven and welcomed him warmly. "Rabbi, we have been waiting for you to come for years. God has told us about you, about your great love for the Torah and the word of God and your equally great devotion to the law, to justice and the people. Come. Welcome to the kingdom of heaven."

The rabbi was stunned. Not only was he getting in, but he was being praised by God, blessed be his name, himself! He spoke again to Peter, "You mean that I'm welcome in heaven?"

"Welcome?" said Peter. "You have one of the highest seats in the kingdom."

"Oh," said the rabbi, "may I ask a question?"

"Of course," Peter responded.

"If I'm getting into the kingdom on my holiness and love for the law and justice, do you think I could get someone else into the kingdom on my holiness of life? After all, in the Jewish community the only reason I am holy and just is because of my students. They were the ones who watched me and held me accountable and called me forth to ever greater devotion and faithfulness. Do you think the Almighty, blessed be his name, would let all my students into the kingdom on account of my holiness and devotion to his law?"

Peter thought for a moment and said, "Wait here for a moment and I'll go ask God." Peter went off and wasn't gone long at all. He returned and said, "Rabbi, I can't believe it, but God says yes—all your students may enter on account of your life. Now, welcome to the kingdom of heaven."

But the rabbi paused again. He spoke. "Do you think the Almighty, blessed be his name, would let others into the kingdom of heaven on my account? After all, all good

Jews love the Torah and are dedicated to the study of the scriptures and would love to be able to be a disciple of a rabbi. But they must obey the commandment to be fruitful and multiply, to marry and then to care for those in need. So many people helped my students and myself with bread and shelter, charity and hospitality. Do you think they could come in too?"

Peter responded, "I don't know, wait here." Off he went and soon he was back again, shaking his head. "Rabbi, God says yes again. All those who helped you and your disciples and served your communities may enter on your holiness. Now, come into the kingdom."

"No," the rabbi said, "I have another question."

"Why am I not surprised?" said Peter.

The rabbi said, "In our tradition if one person is holy then the whole nation is saved. After all, when David sinned, all of Israel did penance with him, and when God, blessed be his name, was pleased with David then all the nation flourished and lived in peace and security. Do you think that God would let the whole nation of Israel in on my merits and holiness?"

This time Peter hesitated and said, "This might take some time. Wait here, I'll be back." The rabbi waited and waited and wondered if he had overstepped his bounds with the Almighty. But Peter came back, smiling broadly, and said, "Rabbi, God can't get over how you use the law on behalf of the people. He loves it. Yes, on your holiness, the entire Jewish nation for all of history is welcome in the kingdom. Now, will you come in?"

The rabbi smiled, warming up, "I have another question."

Peter said, "What could you possibly ask now?"

"Well," the rabbi said, "what about the Christians? After all, the only reason the Jews have remained so faithful is because of the persecution and hounding by the Christians all these years. Do you think the Almighty, blessed be his name, would let the Christians in on account of my justice and love of the Torah?"

Peter couldn't believe his ears and shook his head. "Sit down and make yourself comfortable, Rabbi. I know this is going to take a long time." And off he went. The rabbi waited, it seemed endlessly, and Peter still didn't come back. He began to worry. But finally Peter returned, shaking his head. This time he said "No. No, Rabbi. God says no, there is a limit to who can come in under your shadow. The Christians can't come in."

"Why?" the rabbi asked.

"Well," Peter said, "that's what took me so long. God knew that you'd want to have a reason why there is a limit to what your holiness can do, and he had to teach me the answer. God says, 'The Jews are judged on their holiness and their response to the law, the Torah, and the word in their tradition. However, the Christians are not. They are judged on the Spirit and the law of love and the beatitudes that fulfill the old decalogue. Christians are judged on what they did for the poor and how faithfully they loved their enemies and prayed for their persecutors.' So, no, you can't get them in. Now, will you finally come in?"

The rabbi balked and said, "No, I'm not coming in."

"Why?" bellowed Peter.

"Because," the rabbi said, "I am a Jew. And as a Jew, every year at Passover we bless God and lift four cups of wine in his honor and remember his kindness to the house of Israel. But we do not drink the third cup of wine. Instead we pour it into the ground because it commemorates the death of the Egyptians, our enemies. We cannot rejoice in the death of our enemies. I will not come into the kingdom of heaven until I know that my enemies are home, as well. I will wait."

And no matter how hard Peter tried, he could not get the rabbi to come in. So the gate slammed shut.

So, if you are Jewish and you die, don't worry. Besides Peter, the first person you will see at the gate is the old holy rabbi, and he will wave you on in. And if you are Christian, as you go by the old rabbi, he will count off his enemies as they become friends. And when all of us are one, then the old rabbi can go home.

This is the tradition, the practice and the belief of the Jewish community, the understanding of justice from the ancient times preceding Christianity. The story says that we must be courageous and generous just to be human, let alone a reli-

gious person or a Jew or a Christian. And if our religion as
followers of Jesus, the Jew, is based on self-sacrifice and
courageous love, what kind of justice are we called to
practice and witness to in our lives? The essence of religion, that which holds our life together, is worship of the
God who is justice and courage in community. Justice is
for everyone or no one. Justice is not just for us, but it is
universal, extending to all. We are going to be judged on
our practice and understanding of justice, as the holy
rabbi already knows and practices even though he does
not know Jesus. And if that is the depth of meaning of
justice in the law and the prophets, then what does Jesus'
justice look like?

This story catches us off-guard as unconditional love becomes concrete, not abstract or theoretical. The rabbi is loving, even when the person being loved acts selfishly, insen-
sitively, or unjustly, or even with evil intentions. We often
think that unconditional love means we can do anything and
that the other person, or God, will love us anyway. Instead,
unconditional love means that God and we will love, no
matter what, always offering an alternative to the other's
behavior or lack of love.

This rabbi literally becomes the living torah, the shalom
of God. Shalom means wholeness, justice, peace, holiness,
welcome, invitation, oneness, unity, completeness. The word
shalom encompasses all these meanings and the experience
of these realities. If we are just, as the rabbi in the story is
just, then we know what peace is. We find our peace and
wholeness in the justice of the poor, the wholeness and welcome of the poor and those who are the victims of injustice.
Paul VI says that if we want peace, then we must work for
justice.

The vision of the Messiah was the hope and belief of the
Jewish people in the coming of the presence of justice in their
midst. They believed this presence of justice would be so
strong that they themselves, the people of this Messiah,
would be a light to the nations, a harbor of peace in the world,
and that all would give glory to the God of the Jews because
justice and peace dwelled in their midst. Today, John Paul II
says that if we want peace, we must go to the poor.

The story of the rabbi reminds us forcefully of community and of the people. Our holiness, the rabbi's holiness, is not for the individual. It is for the salvation and hope of the people, all people. The primary focus of our relationship of love with God is others: How many people can we squeeze into our hearts as they expand with the experience of being loved by God? How many people can we give to and share with what we passionately desire, long for, and stake our lives on? How many people will we let tell of the vision before we take it for ourselves?

This old story speaks first of the generosity of the old Jewish law, the code of Israel, and the expansive nature of justice in the Hebrew scriptures. Jesus is a Jew; he grows up with this generosity of belief. All his love and generosity are based on this law of generosity and community. As Christians we grow into the Jewish understanding of justice and mercy and then, hopefully, are converted to Jesus' way of the cross and justice.

We Christians might say that this rabbi acts like Jesus. But the Jews would maintain that this is what it means to be a Jew. What does justice mean for us specifically as Christians? Where is the spirit of this law of justice in Christian belief? The Jewish community is a mirror that reflects back to us the heritage of our beliefs and calls us to account for what we do. We don't always look good in this mirror.

If Jesus had told this story, this parable, to his Jewish contemporaries, how would they have reacted? What about the Romans who were waiting at heaven's gate? What if the Jews couldn't go home to the kingdom until all the Romans had entered? What then? How would Jesus' disciples, Peter, James and John, the sons of thunder, and the others have reacted?

Jesus' parables affected those who heard them, and they are supposed to affect us. They are intended to stun us into reevaluating our positions, our enemies, our love and practice of justice. What if it is our enemies who are waiting— those of certain nations, or, closer to home, child molesters, people we abhor and consider our enemies, enemies of our culture, enemies of human dignity? The story of the rabbi reveals the criterion for justice based in the Hebrew scriptures.

So what is the criterion for justice in the Christian scriptures? All the parables seek to answer that question. What is it to be among the children of God, the brothers and sisters of Jesus, the Christians? Does our God deal with us justly or mercifully? If we were all to die today in an earthquake or nuclear disaster, and we all came before the Son of Man and were seen clearly and truthfully for who and what we are, would we want this Son of Man to deal with us justly or mercifully? This question works its way throughout all the parables.

Do we want God to deal with us mercifully if it means being merciful to others in our lifetime? Or would we rather God deal with us justly, as justly as we deal with others in our lifetime? Mercy goes beyond justice. Although we want God to deal with us mercifully, we usually seek justice for all other people. We begin with justice and hope our way toward mercy. But we *will* be judged as we judge and do justice to others.

For the prophets, justice is one thing; justice in love, reconciliation, and the cross is still another matter. This latter form of justice is developing in liberation theologies throughout the universal church as its members are faced with persecution and struggle.

So, what is justice in Christian terms? Let's look at another of Matthew's parables, the parable of the laborers in the vineyard, for a look at relationships in the kingdom. We need to remember that for Jesus relationships were important—blood relationships and, more so, relationships created by the waters of baptism and belief. When Jesus is approached and told that his mother and brothers and sisters are outside waiting for him, he responds by looking around at his disciples and asking, "Who is my mother? Who are my brothers and sisters?" Then he pointed to his disciples and said, "Look! Here are my mother, my brothers and my sisters. Whoever does the will of my Father in Heaven is my brother, my sister, and my mother" (Matthew 12:48-50; Mark 3:31-35; Luke 8:19-21).

The kingdom is relational, binding beyond ancestry and family, binding in obedience and response to the word of

God and the blood of the cross and Eucharist. Intimacy in the kingdom of God comes from hearing and obeying the will of God and making it come true, incarnating it in history now. Mary is holy, a disciple, not only or primarily because she is the mother of God but because she has heard the word of God, believed in it and put it into practice, incarnating it in her very flesh and blood. That is why in the Eastern churches she is called the Theotokos, the God-bearer. She brings the Word and she bears the presence of God in Jesus to the earth, and we are called to follow in her footsteps of belief and discipleship. We are to bear God to one another; this is what forms the society that Jesus announces and describes in the parables.

■ *"A landowner went out early to hire workers for his vineyard. The workers accepted the salary offered, a piece of silver for the day, and he sent them to his vineyard.*

He went out again at about nine in the morning, and as he saw men idle in the square, he said to them: 'You, too, go to my vineyard and I will pay you what is just.' So they went.

The owner went out at mid-day and again at three in the afternoon, and he did the same. Finally he went out at the last working hour and he saw others standing there. So he said to them: 'Why do you stay idle the whole day?' They answered: 'Because no one has hired us.' The master said: 'Go and work in my vineyard.'

When evening came, the owner of the vineyard said to his manager: 'Call the workers and pay them their wage, beginning with the last and ending with the first.' Those who had come to work at the last hour turned up and were given a denarius each (a silver coin). When it was the turn of the first, they thought they would receive more. But they, too, received a denarius each. So, on receiving it, they began to grumble against the landowner.

They said: 'These last hardly worked an hour, yet you have treated them the same as us who have endured the day's burden and heat.' The owner said to one of them: 'Friend, I have not been unjust with you. Did we not agree on a denarius a day? So take what is yours and go. I want to give to the last the same

*as I give to you. Do I not have the right to do as I please with
my money? Why are you so envious when I am kind?'*
  So will it be: the last will be first, the first will be last" (Matthew 20:1-16).

This parable of the vineyard owner and his workers and
foreman centers on the description of the reign of God. Any
reign is about power, including God's reign. The reign of the
United States has to do with power, with violence, with stat-
ing who we are unequivocally for others' benefit and with
authority. What is the reign of the United States like? I studied this parable with a group of international students only
days after the United States sent a retaliatory force against
Iraq. This was a show of force, intended to teach a lesson
and to assert indignation; it was also a warning of what could
come upon them. But God's reign is about power, authority,
and an absolute *abhorrence* of violence in history; it is about
how those who submit to God's reign practice peace and justice.

The reign in England, from the royal family and the court
down through the lords and ladies and the people of the
realm, is about class and hierarchy, behavior and place. The
reign of God is about hierarchy, too, about structure and class,
but the structure is upside down, with the masses of people,
the sparrows, the poor, the lilies of the field holding the
power. The power base is in the lowly ones. The more power
one has in this reign, this realm, the more one is required to
become a servant to others. It is a class of downward mobility in imitation of Jesus, who came down from heaven to
become human and dwell among us in the small ones of
earth.

Those of us submitting to the reign of God are called to
reflect the values and morality of that kingdom. In a reign
everything is political. And this is no different in the kingdom of heaven. Liturgy, spirituality, ministry, catechetics, religious community, the structures of the church—all are political and reveal how power operates among those in the
community of God, the Body of Christ. That is why the
prophet Amos critiques all the countries around Israel, rip-
ping them to shreds, and saving the best until last: Israel.

The kingdom is about authority and discipline, learned from others and sensed inwardly as the core of belief and practice.

There is a story about this concept in the kingdom.

■ Once upon a time there was a boy who loved horses. He got a job working with horses at a stable, and he spent his time grooming them, exercising them and riding them. It was fantastic, like being in heaven for him.

One day he was sitting on the fence watching a trainer with one of the thoroughbreds on the track. The owner of the stables and track was standing beside him watching the trainer put the horse through his paces. First he'd let the reins out, and the horse would bolt, running like the wind. Then he would pull the reins in as tight as he could, and the horse would almost stop in its tracks. Then he would ease up and let the horse run free, and again pull the reins back hard. He did this again and again until the horse was dancing, prancing and lathered in a thick sweat.

The boy watched the horse and trainer, watched the reins, the bridle and the bit, and became more and more angry. Finally he turned to the owner and said, "That man is abusing that horse. He is not thinking about the horse and its possibilities and capabilities but only about his own power and how far he can push that horse, how much control he has over that animal. He's not thinking about the horse and its limitations."

The owner didn't say anything for a moment, and then he looked at the young man and said, "It's obvious that you know nothing about horses or, for that matter, about discipline."

The boy did a double take. "What do you mean?" he said.

The owner replied, "A good horse, like that thoroughbred, runs at even the shadow of authority. A good horse runs at even the intimation of a command. The difference between a horse and a thoroughbred like this one is the trainer who triggers the internal authority of the horse. The horse does not run to win or even in obedience to the trainer. The horse knows the trainer and the trainer knows that the horse runs because it is a horse. It's obvious that you know very little about horses, about discipline or obedience. What a pity."

And with that, the owner left the boy on the fence, watching the horse from a distance.

Our reactions to the parable and to the story above are usually very negative. The reign of God is about authority, about discipline, about commands and obedience? Do we run at the very shadow of authority, at the intimation of a command? If so, whose? Do we respond like this? Do we obey anyone? Daniel Berrigan says, "I have spent my whole life looking for someone to obey." He also says, "If you're going to be a Christian, you'd better look good on wood." These two statements are intimately connected. Our reactions to the parable and to the words of Dan Berrigan are similar. We want the kingdom to come, and we want to be a part of it, but we could do without the discipline, the authority and the obedience. But the reign of God does have to do with reins, checks and holds that trigger our internal discipline, that touch the essence of who we are and why we run, because we are human.

Let's look at how we would feel if we were in the different groups represented in the parable.

What if we are in the group that was hired last and paid first? Well, we know that the owner controls everything, but that's not so bad. We certainly got more than we bargained for or even dreamed of, and we got it first! The others had to wait in line in the heat, tired and worn out. In fact, we may not quite want to look any of them in the eye. We feel uncomfortable about our good fortune.

But if we began early and worked all day, we are undoubtedly angry and perhaps hurt at the actions of owner. We feel we should be treated according to how much we did. We want our value as workers recognized and rewarded. We did the most; we should get the most. We were the first chosen; we must be the best among the workers. The owner's generosity is infuriating. We may even reflect on the actions of this strange owner and begin to worry about his effect on the status quo. He is, after all, undermining all our assumptions about work, pay, economics, about relations within the community. Even though the owner fulfilled the letter of the contract, we seethe at the injustice we believe has been done to us.

If we were in one of the middle groups, we may just feel uncertain. We got more than we expected, but we also worked more than others who received just as much. We feel lucky, but not as lucky as we could have been. We may also feel a little guilty when we think of those who worked longer than we did.

One feeling runs through all the groups: we have a feeling that things didn't work out fairly. And in the eyes of the world, that is true. Again, the parable turns our usual way of looking at things upside down. The kingdom of God does not have the same values as our world of business and finance. In God's kingdom, this vineyard, this owner keeps going out again and again to gather workers to him. He seeks the idle, the lost, those involuntarily unemployed as well as those who are strong and healthy and looking to better their positions. The day is long, the work is hard and the vines must be picked if there is to be wine in the kingdom. But the wine will be shared with all, *especially* those who are usually forgotten and excluded from the rejoicing and the human qualities of living in this world.

The owner is God, and God makes no deals according to what we may have in mind. God cares for the laborers, all of them. Reality and power are upside down in this kingdom. Individuality and self-worth and deals don't work. What we do does not get us into the kingdom; we are part of the kingdom due solely to the generosity of God. All we can do is respond with gratitude. Everything is based on need and those in greatest need. Justice is love expressed in terms of the sheer human needs that we all share, whether we want to admit it or not. This kingdom is about relationships between the owner and the laborers, among the laborers themselves. It reminds us of our relationships with God and with those who are old, sick, handicapped, poor, disadvantaged, discriminated against for any reason—those who fall through the cracks in society. These are the privileged ones in God's community. They come first.

The parable reveals this question: Do we want this privileged human relationship with God now, or do we want to wait until later, when we are painfully conscious of our needs, our isolation and our separateness from God and others? Do we want this kind of relationship with God while we are still able-bodied? If this is how God treats those in need, how will God relate to those who are gifted, young, healthy, capable, with power, imagination, possibilities and energy? God needs the grapes picked for the wine of the kingdom. God needs those who can help to make the wine of life a reality for others.

Do we want to follow God's foreman as disciples, trusted followers who obey God always, even when opposition rears its ugly head and others decide they don't believe in God's vision, God's realm? What will the foreman get, the disciples get, besides the wine of the kingdom and the trust of the vineyard owner? A great deal of grief, rejection, persecution. And yet the only thing we really know about our master is what we hear from the foreman, what we learn from the foreman's obedience to the will of the owner. The foreman takes risks for us in obedience to the owner. Indeed, this foreman will die so that all might know dignity, that those outcast, lost and cast aside might be gathered first; and that those expecting the best and more will wait on the latest into the vineyard so that they might learn some compassion, some solidarity with others. If we do not deal with this foreman, this one who obeys, and become like him, what then do we really know of the owner of the vineyard, the householder, the one who owns this kingdom, this realm into which we are being called?

If we want to continue to deal with the owner according to covenant and contract alone, God will honor our choice, but then we will not know God's graciousness, tender regard and special compassion. If we want to continue making deals with God, one on one, taking our chances individually, without recourse to the community, God will honor our decision, but then again we will never know the sense of gratitude and overwhelming generosity and intimacy of that last group. And if we choose to embrace the kingdom and accompany the least of our brothers and sisters, as our foreman Jesus has done, then we will be God's beloved children, brothers and sisters to Jesus. The kingdom of Jesus' God is built on this last group, the least among us. The way we treat the least of our brothers and sisters indicates our relationship and intimacy with God. God has made the poor, the least of the earth, the criteria of authority, power and love in this kingdom of justice. God as trinity, as community, aligns with the poor—downward mobility of the incarnation, the option for the poor or, as it is called now in most of the third-world churches, the fundamental imperative of the gospel and the kingdom of heaven.

What is the parable telling us? What must we do to be accepted into the kingdom? First, we need to leave behind the world's assumptions and all that we have worked out individually and come live in solidarity, in friendship, in shared hope and need. And we must ask, ask to come in. We all must change, must shift base no matter what group we find ourselves in at the moment. All are called to conversion, massive radical change and transformation to enter into the group and to live with the others. It is the owner who gives dignity and a sense of meaning to the bottom group, an acknowledgment of their privilege. Together, we become a people because of God's choice, God's calling and going out to seek after us, again and again.

God became human and came among us and died at the bottom. This choice and life of incarnation and death and resurrection is what gives this group of the poor and least their dignity and power and worth—the presence of God remains most clearly with them. We can get into this group by choice or by "falling from grace" (in the world's view)—by losing a job, by getting ill, by losing our possessions, by sin, by any number of mistakes. This group joined Jesus and followed him because of the good news, the hope proffered and the announcement that God is looking after us all. Conversion to the gospel is the entrance way into the group and what allows us to stay—a commitment to continual radical conversion in a community that holds us accountable. We are converted to the living and dying of Jesus in our midst and the living out of this belief is our worship expressed not only ritually in the telling of the stories and the breaking of the bread and the sharing of the wine, but the daily wage, the daily life of solidarity with the least of our brothers and sisters, waiting on the poor and the needy and allegiance to the foreman and obedience to the owner of the vineyard. We live to pick grapes for the wine and to make sure that the wine belongs to those who need it most.

Basically there are four values, four criteria for baptism, for entrance into this community (for any sacrament, for that matter): personal intent to join; knowledge of what we are doing and what the group believes; acceptance and understanding of that belief, its responsibilities and privileges; and conversion and acceptance of the community, which then holds newcomers accountable in its daily life. The relationships internally as well as the persecution and rejection and violence outside mitigate against the community surviving. Constant conversion is what keeps the bottom group alive— in following Jesus and sharing the relationship with others generously. Then we can call God our Father.

Entrance into this group entails justice, restitution, restoration of the balance and inequality due to injustice and then, "half of all we have" to the poor, the bottom group. This is the intent and backdrop of Lent every year, to recall us to our baptismal promises. The liturgy follows the good news and the practice of the kingdom coming, the will of the owner of the vineyard, the householder. This good news and acceptance of the announcement of this kingdom, this realm, demands allegiance to the poor, for the good news comes strongest to them in their deepest needs.

Anyone who has lived among the poor, the least, knows that they endeavor to take care of one another with their limited resources, even those who barge in on them, and supposedly care for them and minister to them. They form a community of necessity. All community is based, in fact, on perceived need. Not to perceive the need keeps the community from developing. There are many other things that militate against community: individualism, materialism, nationalism, violence, greed, and so on. The parables say that the poor exist because of our lifestyle of indifference and insensitivity and individual or communal choices. The primary experience of poverty is not fitting in the existing system.

There are three kinds of poverty. The first kind of poverty is an affront to God, to the human condition. It is forced. It is structural. It is systematic. People are born into it, fall into it or are forced into it. It is the product of war, oppression, nationalism, racism, economic structures, human sin and evil. It is the poverty that rules in this society. It rules in the Third World. It rules in the ghetto and at border crossings. It rules in single-parent families and on reservations. It is the lack of food, shelter, medicine and health care, work, choices and options, a future, education and human dignity.

The second kind of poverty occurs when individuals and groups make themselves poor in the context of the kingdom of heaven, poor for the kingdom, the option for the poor, the fundamental imperative of the gospel. Blessed are the poor in spirit and blessed are those who are persecuted in the cause of uprightness; the kingdom of heaven is already theirs. These two beatitudes are in the present tense. All the others are in the future tense, promises. These are guarantees. We can get into the kingdom of heaven by making ourselves poor for and with others and by being persecuted for justice's sake, because of our work for the gospel. Alignment with the poor—imitating God and throwing in our lot with the poor— ushers us into the kingdom.

When Jesus invites the rich young man into his company, he commands him to go and sell all that he has and give it to the poor, lay up treasure in the kingdom of heaven and then come back and join in the kingdom here, in the company of the disciples, preaching the good news (Mark 8). That is the starting point for the option of the poor. We go and sell what we have but don't immediately need, and we share it with the poor, making relationships with them, making them our friends. It is sharing our resources; we fill up what is lacking in them, and they fill up what is lacking in us. Our single-hearted belief in God, justice and hope in the kingdom starts with this choice, this sharing, this outreach to others in need. Then we find out that they give in return joy, endurance, faithfulness, family, support, laughter, song, community.

The third kind of poverty is the virtue of poverty, which all Christians are called to practice in their daily lives. The vow of poverty, even in a religious community, can fall under this practice of the virtues, especially when the practice and experience is singular and not necessarily connected to an alternative life and witness to the existing dominant society and culture. Or it can fall under the option for the poor, the choice for the kingdom of heaven now, if it is practiced in conjunction with the poor and as witness to another belief and hope and in service to those in need. This vow is practiced together as prophetic witness against injustice and in solidarity with those who are the victims of injustice. The virtue calls all of us to let go of what we don't need, the "security blanket" that allows us to be insensitive to others' needs.

A good deal of the initial practice of the virtue of poverty is connected to material possessions, reputation, connections, lifestyle, choice of neighborhood, job and social status, the existing structure, even within the church. Anything that distances us from people and makes us more independent stands against the virtue of poverty. Anything that enables us to ignore our utter dependence on God destroys poverty and community, because the one thing guaranteed to help us remember and practice our utter dependence on God is our utter dependence on the community of the poor and other people.

We worry that if we go and sell everything we have and give it to the poor, then we'll be destitute. We fear no one will take care of us. But who has taken care of us since the beginning? God and other people, sometimes strangers. The virtue and practice of poverty work against our selfishness and independence and lack of community. All the parables emphasize this aspect of the kingdom. Money, security and protection are the areas where we do not trust God. Our concern reveals to us how little we depend on God, how little we believe in God.

Entrance into the kingdom demands that we who choose to live in God's kingdom subscribe to the values of Jesus. We must be converted to dependence on God and interdependence on one another in community, a community of shared need and shared human dignity. To choose poverty for the kingdom is hard, but it is just as hard, if not harder, to choose poverty for the kingdom and shared hope. It is especially hard for those who have only known enforced poverty, violence and repression in life, as the least of the brothers and sisters have experienced. It is a gift and a privilege to choose the fundamental imperative of the poor. Our first choice is Jesus, the poor one of God, hidden in the midst of the poor, our community.

An old English tale states all this in another way:

■ Once upon a time there was a great forest. It ranged over hills for miles all the way to the western seas. One day one of the great standing trees, an oak, was having a conversation with an elegant, tall pine. As they often did, they talked about the other trees, life in the forest, the weather and all the news that the birds brought with them from the outside. Mostly they spoke of the other trees.

The oak mentioned the lovely, delicate azalea with its pink, soft white and lavender blooms. God certainly knew what he was doing when he made such a creature. Then the pine said, "And look at that rowan tree. Its shade and branches, its smell, and it is so easily carved and made into other beautiful things. Such a creation." They went through the trees one by one, and then the oak nearly spit out, "And look at that ash tree. I just don't know why God created that tree. And there are so many of them! They seem to sprout up everywhere and endure hardily, but they really are rather useless. They burn quickly, and the wood is so soft that it can't be made into other things. It's such a shame there are so many of them."

Days later a woodsman came through the forest looking for a tree. He needed to make something. His house and workshop were falling to ruin. He spoke finally to the great trees, the oak and the pine, for in those days humans and trees and animals could still talk to one another. He asked their suggestions on what tree to choose. They conferred and quickly said, "Take an ash tree. There are so many of them."

And so he did. He chopped the nearest ash tree down and went home. There he made an axe handle for his new blade and then returned to the forest and started swinging. One by one the trees were felled. Down they all went:

the azaleas, the hardwoods, the rowans, the hickory. Finally, he drew near to the oak and the pine, and they realized rather late what was going to happen to them. The oak ruefully spoke his thoughts aloud to the pine and said, "Pine, we made a mistake. We forgot something basic in our quick giving away of the life of the ash tree. We are all trees at root, and the death of one means the death of all of us."

And with those words echoing in the air, the woodsman started on the trunk of the great oak with his new axe with its ash handle.

5

The Sheep and the Shepherd

———— ■ ————

Matthew continues to push home the idea of choosing the poor, of allegiance with the least. He describes the kingdom of heaven as encompassing and embracing the poor as the privileged place of the presence of God, with Jesus in our midst as brother and sister. Jesus' God seeks out these outcasts, these sinners, and the many people society considers expendable. God expects the followers of Jesus to do the same. Worship, liturgy and daily life must all dovetail together in one piece where these people are befriended, aided, given hospitality, hope and an equal share in the blessings of the kingdom. This is the basis of justice in the kingdom, and it will be the basis of judgment, salvation and our place in the kingdom when it comes in its fullness.

The image of the shepherd appears often in scripture. David the king was first a shepherd. And Matthew's genealogy of Jesus begins, "A family record of Jesus Christ, son of David." Jesus comes from a family of shepherds. Indeed, when King Herod asks his priests and scribes where the Messiah is to be born, they quote Micah 5:1, "This is what the prophet wrote: *And you, Bethlehem, land of Judah, you are by no means the least among the clans of Judah, for from you will come a leader, the one who is to shepherd my people Israel"* (Matthew 2:5-6). The old writings are rife with images of the people as sheep and lambs and the one to come as the shepherd. Isaiah describes the child in the readings of Christmas Midnight Mass:

For a child is born to us,
a son is given us;
the royal ornament is laid upon his shoulder,
and his name is proclaimed:
"Wonderful, Counselor, Divine Hero,
Everlasting Father, Prince of Peace."

To the increase of his powerful rule
in peace, there will be no end.
Vast will be his dominion,
he will reign on David's throne
and over all his kingdom,
to establish and uphold it
with justice and righteousness
from this time onward and for ever.

The zealous love of Yahweh Sabaoth will do this.

This is the child who smashes the rod of the peoples' task-master and lifts the yoke that burdens them and the pole on their shoulder (Isaiah 9:5-6, 3-4). This is our God! Later in Isaiah there is a cry of announcement and warning:

Go up onto the high mountain, messenger of Zion,
lift up your voice with strength,
fear not to cry aloud when you tell Jerusalem
and announce to the cities of Judah:
Here is your God!
Here comes your God with might;
his strong arm rules for him;
his reward is with him,
and here before him is his booty.
Like a shepherd he tends his flock:
he gathers the lambs in his arms,
he carries in his bosom,
gently leading those that are with young (Isaiah 40:9-11).

The shepherd is a protector, a wall of strength and security for the sheep. Jesus himself, the Messiah, is described as the suffering one, led like a lamb to the slaughter (Isaiah 53).

The image of the lamb has echoes that are strong and evocative for the Israelites, who took the blood of the Passover lamb and smeared it on their doorposts so the Angel of Death would pass over their household and let their children live. The blood of the sacrificed one, slaughtered and shared in a meal of remembrance, is the foundation of freedom and hope for the chosen ones, saved from oppression and slavery.

Halfway through his gospel, Matthew has Jesus speak to his disciples on their way up to Jerusalem: "See that you never despise one of these little ones. I assure you, their angels in heaven constantly behold my heavenly Father's face." He then challenges them with a parable.

■ *"A man owns a hundred sheep and one of them wanders away; will he not leave the ninety-nine out on the hills and go in search of the stray? If he succeeds in finding it, believe me he is happier about this one than about the ninety-nine that did not wander away. Just so, it is no part of your heavenly Father's plan that a single one of these little ones shall ever come to grief"* (Matthew 18:12-14).

The little ones, the lowly (as Mary describes herself) those of no account, expendable, the least, not counted, uncared about, shunted to the side, these are the first of the children of God. This image of the children of God includes all those in society without power, not primarily or only children. Jesus clearly demonstrates to his disciples in this same chapter of Matthew that they are to become like these little ones if they are to enter into his kingdom, for they are of the greatest importance in that heavenly reign (Matthew 18:4).

The groups, of course, are a never-ending litany of the masses of people in the human community: the one-third of the human race that at any one time is homeless, landless, without a country, migrant, on the move. The least are those not protected by law, not included in systems of health care or education, not given shelter and basic care. They are those who fall through the cracks in nations, organizations and church. The lowly are those who have no say in the decision-making processes, no political clout, no access to money; a very unstable future and insecurity are their norms.

Simply put, they are the poor, desperate for anyone to notice them, treat them as human beings with dignity, to offer the tenderness and regard of the corporal works of mercy, the acts of hands-on-flesh justice. The corporal, bodily works of mercy are the long-term, continually needed resources and practices of providing food, drink, clothing, shelter, medical care, supportive presence, freedom—a life of more than just surviving daily. The corporal works of mercy, then, deal with the hungry, the thirsty, the naked, the homeless, the sick, the imprisoned and lastly the dead, in need of burial and a last act of dignity, giving them back to the earth. These are the poor that Jesus' good news is primarily and first proclaimed to and given to as hope, as mainstay, as lifeline, especially when it is made flesh and blood in a community.

The parable in Matthew begins with an exhortation: "See that you never despise one of these little ones!" This is not light language, but a harsh warning, confrontation and conviction. Not a one is to be despised. Earlier, in chapter 10 of Matthew's gospel Jesus uses the image of the sparrow to startle people:

■ *"For only a few cents you can buy two sparrows, yet not one sparrow falls to the ground with your Father's consent. As for you, every hair of your head has been counted. So do not be afraid; you are worth much more than many sparrows.*

Whoever acknowledges me before the people of the earth I will acknowledge before my Father in Heaven. Whoever rejects me before the people of the earth I will reject before my Father in Heaven" (Matthew 10:29-33).

This is continued in very specific terms in the discourse on the mission of the disciples and how the friends and followers of Jesus are to treat all others: "And I promise you if anyone gives even a cup of cold water to one of these little ones, because he is a disciple of mine, he will not go unrewarded" (Matthew 10:42). These lowly, these little ones are priceless to Jesus, to the Father and the Spirit, who hold them in their heart. We also must learn to do so if we are believers in this household of heaven here on earth.

The punch of the parable is in that image of the sparrow, of those little ones that the powerful of the world, the systems and structures of the dominant culture and the self-sufficient of the earth don't even know are there and don't care one whit about in daily practice.

■ *"What did you think of this? If a man has a hundred sheep and one of them strays, will he not leave the ninety-nine on the hills to go and look for the stray one?" (Matthew 18:12).*

No way! Leave the ninety-nine to marauders, thieves, wolves? No way! We might notice the one and curse silently about the stupidity of the dumb sheep, but we are not about to go traipsing off and leave the others all alone. But Jesus does go off, leaving all the others, and eventually does find the one that led him on a wandering chase through briars and brambles, ravines and rocks. And he rejoices more over this dumb sheep than all the others he left behind! The world does not operate like this! It operates in the exact opposite way! That is the heart of the issue. Jesus and Jesus' God are shepherds of whole peoples over history; they shepherd all the masses of people in the world's nations with the Spirit to find the wandering and lost and those who don't stay with the ones in the structures. Just as one sparrow's loss does not go unnoticed, no straying sheep is abandoned, and not one of these least among the earth's peoples is forgotten or uncared for. God rejoices over these little ones, these lost ones, these least and forgotten more than all the others who, left to themselves, took care of themselves.

Now it's time for a story to set the stage for the scriptures and to get us thinking about judgment: ours, and all those who call themselves Christians and the rest of the world too. This story is from the Middle Ages, and there are versions of it in both eastern and western Europe.

■ Once upon a time there was a nasty old woman. She hadn't always been old, of course, but people thought she had. It was the way she acted. She had had a terrible life. She never had a home. She lived on the streets. She survived by stealing food and eating out of the garbage, begging and shoving everyone else aside so that she could get the best that was thrown out and discarded by others. There was not an ounce of human kindness in her body. She wailed and flailed her way through the streets and the dump. She was always moaning and groaning, complaining and finding fault with everyone, including those who gave to her when she begged from them, even the ones who were generous and tried to ease her life. Her life was hard, but she was a real pain.

Then she died. She got to the pearly gates and found that God himself, the Almighty, was waiting for her with his arms folded and a very stern countenance. She came up, brash as ever, and said, "Well, are you going let me in?" And God said, "No." "What do you mean, you're not going to let me in? They told us down there that if we were miserable on earth then we'd get a good place in here, in heaven."

God said, "I know they say that, but it just isn't true. That's not the way it works." She was indignant. "You've got to let me in. My life was so terrible. I deserve happiness." And God just kept shaking his head. "In order to get in here, there has to be some sort of human kindness, some goodness in your life, and we can't find anything." "What do you mean 'we'?" And God replied, "I have all the angels in the back room looking through the records, the books of anything you ever did, said, looked at, intended, thought about doing, anything at all, even dreamed about, and we can't find one single good thing!"

That sobered her a little, and she began to panic. Then one by one the angels started checking in and every one of them just shook its head and wings and walked away saying, "Nothing" and leaving its book on the table. Finally, one angel, very bedraggled, came in carrying a dirty, ragged piece of carrot—the worst looking carrot ever seen. He held up the carrot before God and said, "This is it. This is the only thing we can find."

God looked at the carrot and said, "That's it?" "Yes," said the angel, "it seems that long ago, one night when she was rooting through the garbage and taking whatever was edible, this was the one piece she left for someone else. This one may get her in." God looked askance at the carrot but took it and handed it to her. She asked, "What are you giving me that ugly looking thing for—I didn't want to eat it even while I was on earth!" "Listen," God said, "this carrot may get you into the kingdom of heaven. Stop complaining, take the carrot."

She took the carrot and she started rising off the ground! She rose higher and higher. She could see the gates of heaven off in the distance. The carrot was carrying her home! She broke into a big grin and thought, "Great, I'm getting in!" She got more and more ecstatic. And as she drew nearer the gates, she thought, "My life on earth was terrible, but it is getting me in forever. I think I'll look down at earth one last time, for a last glimpse."

And as she looked down at earth, from heaven's vantage point, she was amazed to see that a dirty old bum was hanging onto her skirt! He was hanging on for dear life, and there was another one hanging onto his trouser leg and another and another. There was this long trail, a long line of people strung out behind her, all the way down to earth, riding in on her carrot! And she was angry. She started shaking and kicking and squirming around to shake loose the bum who had her skirt tightly grasped in his grubby hand. She started screaming, "Let go of me, this is my carrot!" She was screaming at the top of her lungs and shaking, and the carrot brought her closer and closer to the gates. When she was just within reach of the gate, she yelled one more time, "It's *my* carrot!" And not thinking, she let go of the carrot and hit the person hanging onto her. She fell, and everyone else fell all the way down, down, down to hell. And as she fell, God looked at the angels and said, "Well, at least at the end she told the truth. It was just her carrot."

This story doesn't warm our hearts. It's too close to home. Even if we laugh, we soon ruefully reflect and feel a bit of guilt and perhaps even some remorse. It leads to a hard examination of conscience. God gave the old woman one more chance, and she still blew it. God is just, but God's mercy is beyond belief. Again and again God offers hope, a chance to change, to acknowledge who we are and where we have come from, as well as what we have done with what has been entrusted to us in our lives. What we do all throughout life is probably what we're going to continue doing in heaven, or at least, at the gates.

Some people say this is a human story, not a story that God would tell! Oh, yes he does. Think of the parable of the lost son. The father keeps giving both sons another chance, trying again and again to get them both into the house at the same time, reconciled with each other and with the father. The story ends with the father pleading with the older brother to come in. Then the father goes back into the party with the younger brother, leaving the other brother out in the field, with us, to decide whether or not we're going to come in. This story is not so different, really. It is disconcerting because it says not everybody gets in to heaven, and not everybody who claims to be a believer or know God and God's ways gets in either. Obviously, something else operates in judgment besides knowing God. Others must experience that knowing of God as expressed in their lives, their sharing and their relationships with others.

Some folks say that they believe everyone starts out good and that it's hard to believe that they're not that way at the end too—all of us. Is there anyone we would prefer *not* to spend eternity with in heaven? Most of us could list some individuals and groups, people from history and from our own lives. At least, we would prefer not to know where they are or be assured that their mansion is way out in the sticks away from where ours are located. What kind of people do we have trouble knowing share the kingdom of heaven with us, forever? We usually respond with humor, but we see the question as a question of justice. If there is going to be justice, then people will have to be held accountable, held responsible for what they did or didn't do on earth. The question of judgment and salvation has to do with whether or not God is just. For those who have experienced injustice all their lives, they want justice done; some sort of acknowledgment, restitution and righting of the balance.

A woman, worn and broken, once said to me: "At least at judgment, justice will be done. I buried my daughter, my son-in-law, my husband and four other members of my family. They had all been tortured by government security forces and paramilitary groups. I go to church and see some of the killers there, going to communion and acting like what they do has no consequences." This is a grave incident, yet others have touched this sort of drastic injustice. Parents who have seen their children maimed and killed by drunken drivers have to deal with the driving need to see these people in jail for the rest of their lives or executed. If justice is not our experience of life here on earth, there must be a final reckoning, a place where justice is done. Otherwise, we think, God is not just and the whole idea of religion is up for grabs.

We judge one another all the time, and our present behavior indicates how we feel and what we want done: the people we don't talk to, the people we refuse to eat with, the ones we won't associate with or give the time of day to, the ones we won't forgive for some insult or wrong done to us, even if it is only our perception of being wronged. We judge, and God judges. The question is: what are the criteria for the judgments? The list starts to be fleshed out: the self-righteous, the small-minded, those who gossip and ruin others' reputations, those who make conscious evil choices, individually or collectively in laws and systems, in nations and states, from the death penalty to nationalistic wars and the consequences visited upon the innocent and those caught in the crossfire. We are going to be held responsible for the evil in the world: what we have done, what we have contributed to, what we have tolerated or encouraged, what we have ignored and participated in for our own gain. There is much evil in the world, much that is not repented of or restitution made for. We want justice done individually and universally. There must be a reckoning, and the world must know who made faithful choices in the face of unbearable pain and tragedy, who forgave and acted mercifully, who destroyed and existed selfishly. Forgiveness is based on repentance, restitution, and an intent to convert, but it is also conviction and shared justice and mercy. Evil exists in business, politics, families, governments, structures, systems and personal lives. All can be forgiven, but where is justice in this offer of forgiveness?

Do we want God to deal with us justly or mercifully? When God looks at us and thinks about justice and mercy, what is God thinking about? What does the justice of God look like when God looks at us, and what does the mercy of God look like when God looks at us? What is the difference?

Justice in the Jewish community is strong and encompasses relations and actions among themselves as light to the nations. In the Christian community, in the good news, this justice is fulfilled, completed, expanded to encompass all nations, all peoples, even and especially our enemies and those who have done us harm. It becomes deeper and broader, more involving and intense. Mercy evolves also. Justice in the early Jewish law was "an eye for an eye and a tooth for a tooth," which at least limited what could be done in response or retaliation to wrong as it was experienced. It put limits on reactions. But justice is much more than that: "You are to love the Lord your God with all your heart and all your strength and all your soul and all your mind and you are to love your neighbor as yourself." Justice includes the worship and honor of God and its parallel behavior toward others. Jesus extends that justice among his community members to the right treatment of all. Matthew, in Jesus' Sermon on the Mount, states it most clearly:

> "You have heard that it was said: *Love your neighbor and hate your enemy.* But this I tell you: Love your enemies, and pray for those who persecute you, so that you may be children of your Father in Heaven. For he makes his sun rise on both the wicked and the good, and he gives rain to both the just and the unjust.
>
> If you love those who love you, what is special about that? Do not even tax collectors do as much? And if you are friendly only to your friends, what is so exceptional about that? Do not even the pagans do as much? For your part you shall be righteous and perfect in the way your heavenly Father is righteousness and perfect" (Matthew 5:43-48).

Justice tells us how to deal with evil as well as how to respond to the good or the innocent or the least among us.

And mercy in the earlier tradition? God says, You are my chosen people. I will make a covenant with you and I will be faithful and keep you in my heart and I will come after you again and again, leading you back to my heart and teaching you faithfulness through the law and the prophets and my choosing you always. Mercy in the Christian scriptures says, Now *all* are chosen, the least among us, the poor, the widow, the orphan, the illegal alien, the prisoner, the outcast, the slave, servant, the undesirables, the untouchables, the enemy. All these reveal the extent and depth of God's mercy, given to them first. Mercy will be extended to us by how we treat these least among us. Mercy assumes that justice has been done. The practice of justice is a response to the experience of God's mercy in our lives. We begin to live and to hunger and thirst for justice for all when we experience the reality that God has never dealt with us primarily in the form of justice but has been merciful to us from the very beginning—thank God!

If we have ever known the mercy of God, if we have ever realized that we didn't get what we deserved from God, then the only response to this experience of God's mercy is to act justly and begin to walk humbly with our God. And yet, we are not a people known for the justice we extend to others, let alone mercy. The practice and exercise of justice is the religious response to having experienced the mercy of God in our lives. If we have ever been forgiven, let off the hook, given another chance, then the only response to that gift is to live justly, to give to others what is demanded in justice because they are human beings and because when God could have dealt with us justly, he didn't. Instead, he gave us another chance to repent and be converted to the justice of Jesus. We are always forgiven. But if we are going to accept that forgiveness and be reconciled to God and to the community then we must do justice; we must make restitution and restore the balance and mend the wounds caused by our sin, evil and injustice individually and collectively. Reconciliation means "to walk together again with God and one another," and the way we do that is to practice justice.

All this is background for Matthew's story of the last judgment, sometimes called the judgment of the nations. It uses the symbols of shepherd, sheep and the wandering ones, the least in the kingdom, the little ones, the lamb of God who becomes the One long awaited, both sacrifice and salvation, food for the journey and judge for the end times.

■ *"When the Son of Man comes in his glory with all his angels, he will sit on the throne of Glory. All the nations will be brought before him, and as a shepherd separates the sheep from the goats, so will he do with them, placing the sheep on his right and the goats on his left" (Matthew 25:31-33).*

This is the set up. It evokes all sorts of responses when we hear it for the first time in the context of all this talk of sheep and shepherds. Suddenly the question is: Who is this judge, this Son of Man? And the angels are back! And now there are goats as well as sheep, and it's whole nations being judged together, not just individual people! All of a sudden there are unexpected twists to the usual images of judgment day that we have collected from childhood and spiritual reading and stories. We've imagined one-on-one judgment, not public but individual, certainly not communal by nations! Now all the angels of heaven are there—all the angels of the little ones, the least who always stand before and see the face of Jesus' Father and see, watch and care for their charges, a protective presence of the shepherding God. This is judgment: the Son of Man, angels and all the nations of the earth. There are only two groups: sheep and goats. But again, who is this Son of Man?

Daniel tells us:

"I continued watching the nocturnal vision:
    One like a son of man came on the clouds of heaven. He faced the One of Great Age and was brought into his presence.
    Dominion, honor and kingship were given him, and all the peoples and nations of every language served him. His dominion is eternal and shall never pass away; his kingdom will never be destroyed.
    I, Daniel, was deeply troubled, since these visions terrified me" (Daniel 7:13-15).

In later visions, after Daniel prays for the people and God's continued mercy in his covenant, acknowledging that the people have all sinned and deserve to be punished, he stands before God shamefacedly on behalf of the people. He says: "Justice, O Lord, is on your side." Yet he pleads for mercy, relying not on the just deeds of the people but the great mercy of the Lord. Then the angel Gabriel comes in a vision and tells Daniel: "Everlasting justice will be introduced, vision and prophecy ratified, and a most holy will be anointed" (Daniel 9:24b NAB).

Later, the visions become more specific about this one like the Son of Man and what exactly he will do and its effect on the world. The angel speaks again:

> "At that time, Michael will rise, the Great Commander who defends the sons of your people. It shall be a time of anguish as never before since the nations first existed until this very day.
>
> Then all those whose names are written in the Book will be saved. Many of those who sleep in the Region of Dust will awake, some to everlasting life but others to eternal horror and shame. Those who acquired knowledge will shine like the brilliance of the firmament; those who taught people to be just will shine like the stars for all eternity.
>
> And you, Daniel, keep these words secret and have the Book sealed until the appointed time of the end. Many will wander looking here and there. Wickedness will go on increasing" (Daniel 12:1-4).

The Son of Man is judge, the coming promise of justice in the midst of the people, weighing the scales and separating the just from the wicked, favoring the faithful ones and those chosen by God. There are only two choices: live forever, shining brightly like the stars in the firmament, or be an everlasting disgrace. Son of Man is the title or description that Jesus himself most often uses to refer to himself and his vision of who he is and what he is here to do. In all the references to the passion and suffering that face him because of preaching the good news and bringing this kingdom of heaven to earth he calls himself the Son of Man. He adds that the Son of Man will come with his Father's glory, accompanied by his angels, and when he does "he will reward each one according to their deeds" (Matthew 16:24-28). It is both promise and warning; if we are to be the disciples of Jesus, then we begin by denying ourselves, picking up our crosses and following the crucified one, even if we lose everything, even our lives, in the process. If we do this, we will follow him into the glory of the kingdom as well.

The Son of Man has all the shadows of the lamb of sacrifice, slaughtered on behalf of the people, bringing them life, hope of a future, and salvation and the promised land. The Son of Man is also the shepherd who leads them there, going before them carrying his cross and opening the gates of heaven, welcoming and inviting in all who were faithful or who shared his suffering, innocent of the blood of others and in communion with all those who suffered unjustly at the hands of others. The Son of Man comes in glory to judge the nations with justice because the Son of Man suffered as the poor man, the crucified one at the hands of all the peoples. He was innocent, led as a lamb to the slaughter, siding with all the lost sheep, the forgotten and betrayed, the condemned and cast aside. The Son of Man is the least among the children of earth, the sun of justice, the son of justice, the bruised and broken one who came that we might all have life and have it ever more abundantly, the one left outside a city in the garbage dump to die. All those who have experienced injustice at the hands of others find that this One sides with them. He stands by them and lifts them up as the criteria for salvation, for the coming of justice at the end of time and the redemption of their sufferings. He gives them meaning because he is one of them, the least of all the brothers and sisters among the children of God.

The story continues:

■ . . . *placing the sheep on his right, the goats on his left.*
The King will say to those on his right: "Come, blessed of my Father! Take possession of the kingdom prepared for you from

*the beginning of the world. For I was hungry and you fed me, I
was thirsty and you gave me drink. I was a stranger and you
welcomed me into your house. I was naked and you clothed me.
I was sick and you visited me. I was in prison and you went to
see me."*

*Then the upright will ask him: "Lord, when did we see you
hungry and give you food; thirsty and give you drink, or a
stranger and welcome you, or naked and clothe you? When did
we see you sick or in prison and go to see you?" The King will
answer, "Truly, I say to you: whenever you did this to one of
the least, to my brothers and sisters, you did it to me."*

*Then he will say to those on his left: "Cursed people, go away
from me into the eternal fire which has been prepared for the
devil and his angels! For I was hungry and you did not give me
anything to eat, I was thirsty and you gave me nothing to drink;
I was a stranger and you did not welcome me into your house;
I was naked and you did not clothe me; I was sick and in prison
and you did not visit me."*

*They, too, will ask: "Lord, when did we see you hungry,
thirsty, naked or a stranger, sick or in prison, and did not help
you?" The King will answer them: "Truly, I say to you: whatever you did not do for one of the least of these, you did not do
to me."*

*And these will go into eternal punishment, but the just to
eternal life (Matthew 25:31-46).*

Where is love in all this? Is love connected to justice, or is
love connected to ignoring what people do? Love says you
must do something. Love says you do not do evil. Love says
you do not allow others to continue harming other people or
themselves. Love intervenes with injustice and seeks to stop
it in the flesh and in structures and systems and groups. There
is a long way to go in being a Christian; the door is open to
conversion of heart and life, open to grace. But we often say
that basically we are all right, and so we start to die as believers, slipping away from becoming as compassionate or
merciful or perfect as Jesus exhorts his followers to become
in imitation of his own life and the One he follows, the Father of mercy. We are *not* all right, but that's OK. God ac-

cepts us, forgives us and calls us in a church to constant conversion and to becoming more of what we claim to be as the children of God.

We live on the edge all the time, the edge of justice, the edge of mercy and love, the edge of hope, the cutting edge that clears the way for others' life and hope and future because of our practice of the kindest cut of all: that of justice, the practice of justice for all. It can be a moment of grace and insight, of acknowledging the need to repent and not to take for granted the end point and not to take for granted all those people around us in need. They are the blatant presence of God in our midst, asking and begging for acknowledgment, help and care. What we want to do for God, we are invited and even commanded to do for these, the least of our brothers and sisters. What we do or don't do for them, we do or refuse to do for our God. This is God visible in our midst.

But, we say, we can't just open our door to strangers and take in outcasts. That is true. We cannot act primarily as lone rangers. We are called to act in community, together with others as support, backup and affirmation as well as protection and foundation. This is about judgment of the nations, judgment of groups, communities, churches, peoples. It is catholic judgment, universal judgment, based on catholic, universal, communal action on behalf of the least of our brothers and sisters in the world. We only have to deal with fear when we do not have a community to rely on or to share the burden of care. Action on behalf of the poor and the least only becomes a major threat, sometimes with terrifying and destructive consequences, when we have to act alone because society and the community force us to deal individually with this enormous need. We cannot always pass the individual on to an organization or outreach group or government agency. The core of our religion, the core of love, is the practice of the corporal works of mercy. They are the criteria for whether or not we love God. The note in the New American Bible on this text says: "The parables teach that the Christian community is to be ever ready to meet the Lord at his second coming and to function with a sense of personal responsibility for divine gifts received and to be constantly aware of the primacy of love of neighbor." This is what it looks like in practice here on earth: the response of love expressed in giving to others, in justice, what they need to be human with us. Anything that allows us to ignore or to refuse to respond to these needs is not religion, not love, and it will convict us in the end of lack of love, lack of justice and lack of worship of God.

The issue of nations, not just the issue of individual judgment, is more uncomfortable and more difficult to deal with. If we divide the nations into categories of sheep and goats— all Americans, all Cubans, all Canadians, all Irish, all English, all Peruvians, and so on—and lump the citizens into that one group, we become very confused. Americans, for example, comprise less than 5 percent of the world's population, but use more than 82 percent of the world's resources. In terms of gross national product and status in the United Nations and World Bank, Americans are at the very top of the pinnacle. Yet Americans are down around twentieth in countries that give in relation to their GNP even to the United Nations, let alone to church organizations. If all Americans, regardless of religious affiliation, were judged by these criteria of the corporal works of mercy, Americans would be in the goat group (though some people dissent very vehemently and loudly to this judgment).

What about all American Catholics? The total population in the United States is around 250 million people, with Catholics numbering approximately 59 million of them. If all Catholics in the United States were judged on what we have done for the poor, where would we stand? We'd remain with the goats! American Catholics are statistically one of the richest religious groups in the country, and yet our average giving is among the lowest. Budgets for church groups do not put American Catholics up there with the generous in relation to the wealth and access to systems and structures that are available to us as a national church. The budgets and the allotments in specific dioceses show that the poor generally do not fare much better. On an even smaller and more intimate basis, there is the parish. Again, the budgets and agendas and actual practices reflect building maintenance and services, not an emphasis on corporal works of mercy. If as an American, an American Catholic, a member of a particular diocese and a member of a certain parish, we find ourselves in the goat group—fourfold!—what are the possibilities of our jumping the fence into the sheep pen?

I once did the above exercise in a town on the American-Mexican border. The response was marked by the difference of those from either side of the border. Someone said: "Americans are goats. Goats eat anything and everything in sight, leaving nothing in an area and destroying the environment. Their appetites are bottomless, with very few limits on profit making, security, self-sufficiency and getting the best economic deals in trade agreements and raw materials and recruiting a labor force in foreign countries where there are no regulations. They take advantage of injustice and want and poverty to amass more and more without regard to the price and toll it exacts on those within just miles of their borders, let alone those farther away." The silence was awful. But the question is more about American Catholics than any nation. If the nations are to be judged justly using the criterion of what we do for the least among us, then we, as religious believers, followers of Jesus, must look at this parable and its ramifications for liturgy and worship, ministry, spirituality and the practice of morality, virtue and justice in our own parishes, diocese and country.

In other countries the process follows the same road, with perhaps some side trips. In Ireland the statistics offer a breather and some hope; in relation to the gross national product of that very Catholic nation, sharing and giving is of a more generous nature. In addition, the influx of Irish missionaries to poor countries and their return to Ireland keeps the Irish church attentive to the universal needs of the poor, to the issues of justice and charity and to a response based on the gospel.

We must deal with the fact that we have to go home to the kingdom together or not go, and that the criteria will be what we as a group have done for the poor. Each community has to deal with its priorities, values, decision-making processes and inner relationships. If the culture, the society, does not care about the least among us, and if budgets reflect that same lack of concern in dioceses and parishes, where is the church—in the goat category or the sheep pen? Again, if we subscribe to and reflect the cultural and religious values in our life in two or three or four groups of "goats," what are the possibilities of becoming a sheep at the last individual judgment and the last moment? It becomes crucial to know the company we keep, the groups and people we align ourselves with and who among the poor counts us as friend. It becomes apparent that justice must be done, recompense must be made to those who have never had a chance, those who have suffered innocently and unjustly and those who have stood in opposition to those who were selfish, self-sufficient, greedy, insensitive to the plight of others.

If God were to deal with us justly, right now or ever, most of us would not get into the kingdom. So, if we must rely on the mercy of God to get us into the kingdom, we must begin right now in this moment to practice justice as a response of gratitude and thanksgiving (Eucharist). We must examine our priorities and practice justice, so that mercy might be a possibility. In Jesus' community the corporal works of mercy, the befriending of the poor, the work against injustice, the wholehearted commitment to the fundamental imperative of siding with the least of our brothers and sisters, these are the only possibilities until we get to the gates of the kingdom.

Perhaps the story that wraps this all together is from the last add-on chapter in John's gospel. The morning of the resurrection we find Jesus on a beach on the sea of Galilee. The disciples have gone back to their old life: fishing. They've been out all night and haven't caught a fish. Jesus tells them, though they don't recognize him, where the fish are. They come in with a boat full of fish, and Jesus serves them breakfast on the beach, a reconciling and forgiving gesture and celebration. They are companions again.

Afterward Jesus invites Peter for a walk on the beach alone. Thinking how he had denied Jesus, Peter probably didn't want to be alone with him any more than the others who betrayed him and ran and cared only about their own skins and not their friendship with their master and teacher. But they go off down the beach together, and three times Jesus asks Peter, calling him Simon, son of John, if he loves him more than the others do. And three times Peter is adamant that he does. Each time Peter affirms his love, Jesus says, "Then, feed my sheep, take care of my lambs, feed my sheep."

The only penance Peter will ever receive from Jesus is that of taking care of the sheep. Jesus does not treat Peter with justice, but with mercy, going after the one lost sheep. Peter must take care of the lost and those that are seen as expendable and useful only for profit or fodder for war and nations' GNP. Peter must become the shepherd.

The only penance any of us is given after our acceptance of the faithful forgiveness of God is that of taking care of the sheep, the least of our brothers and sisters. What we do for them, God takes personally as what we do for him in our gratitude for mercy's touch. The last words of Jesus to Peter are the first ones: "Follow me!" And so, the gospel ends with Peter as a disciple, starting from scratch again, forgiven, repentant, making restitution and doing justice the rest of his life because of his own need for mercy, mercy, and more mercy. He now walks again with Jesus and his brothers and sisters, reconciled and saved and set on the journey once again to the kingdom.

Jesus didn't say, "Feed the goats," because the goats feed themselves! They have no need of others. Feed the sheep, feed the lambs, take care of the sheep. If we do this, then justice begins to make an inroad into the world even now, and it will come in the fullness of time at judgment. And mercy begins to be an echo, a glimmer like the stars high above us.

■ Once upon a time there was a blacksmith who worked hard at his trade. The day came for him to die. The angel was sent to him, and much to the angel's surprise he refused to go. He pleaded with the angel to make his case before God, that he was the only blacksmith in the area and it was time for all his neighbors to begin their planting and sowing. He was needed. So the angel pleaded his case before God. He said that the man didn't want to appear ungrateful, and that he was glad to have a place in the kingdom, but could he put off going for a while? And he was left.

About a year or two later the angel came back again with the same message: the Lord was ready to share the fullness of the kingdom with him. Again the man has reservations and said: "A neighbor of mine is seriously ill, and it's time for the harvest. A number of us are trying to save his crops so that his family won't become destitute. Please come back later." And off the angel went again.

Well, it got to be a pattern. Every time the angel came, the blacksmith had one excuse or another. The blacksmith would just shake his head and tell the angel where he was needed and decline. Finally, the blacksmith grew very old, weary and tired. He decided it was time, and so he prayed: "God, if you'd like to send your angel again, I'd be glad to come home now." Immediately the angel appeared, as if from around the corner of the bed. The blacksmith said: "If you still want to take me home, I'm ready to live forever in the kingdom of heaven." And the angel laughed and looked at the blacksmith in delight and surprise and said: "Where do you think you've been all these years?" He was home.

6

The Widow and the Unjust Judge

———— ■ ————

The Widow and the Unjust Judge is probably Luke's short-est parable; Jesus' description is simple and to the point. It is a parable on the necessity of praying always and not losing heart. Its opening questions all have to do with assumptions about prayer. Perhaps a story will provide a starting point. This story is from India, a Hindu story about an emperor and a peasant woman and prayer.

■ Once upon a time there was an emperor named Akaba. He was good and just, but every once in a while the bur-dens of being a good and just ruler got to him and he went out hunting for the day. He took his servants and along with his retinue they went hunting. All morning and most of the day they hunted and caught nothing, not even a glimpse of a deer. The emperor was feeling frustrated and annoyed. This was not turning out to be a restful day or even a diversion from his work and duties. He began to take out his feelings on his retinue.

Then the time came for the prayers. As good Muslims, they dismounted the horses and all gathered together for the ritual. They knelt, facing east, with their heads touch-ing the ground. Akaba, even though he was saying his prayers, had a lot of other things on his mind: the worries of the kingdom, his desire to go home with a good deer slung over his horse, a sense of contentment before having to go back and face all those who waited on his authority and power. He was thinking about how infrequently he got away from work, and that Allah, the Compassionate One, was not providing him with game on this day. He blessed Allah but hoped after the prayers that his luck would change and he'd get a chance to catch something.

At the same time, deep in the heart of the forest there was an older woman. She was married, and earlier her husband had gone off into the woods. She was worried because he was gone much longer than he should have been. She loved him dearly and was afraid that something had happened to him. Just at the time that Akaba and his servants knelt to pray on the ground, she decided to go and look for her husband. Soon she was frantic, running in every direction through the forest, backtracking where she had been before and becoming more and more worried. She wasn't watching where she was going in her haste, and she came upon them kneeling in prayer and she fell over the emperor! She got up, paid him no attention and ran on deeper into the forest, looking still for her husband.

Akaba was annoyed even more, but he finished his prayers along with everyone else and then rose to his feet. Immediately, he ordered some of his soldiers to go and find that woman and bring her to him. In the meantime, the woman found her husband and was overjoyed. He was old and not feeling well and needed her help and assistance. He had stumbled and she was helping him back to the house when she was found and dragged back to the emperor. He gave her a good talking to. She should be more concerned about whom she fell over—he was the emperor—didn't she notice that?

She responded, "What were you doing on the ground in the first place?" And he said, "I was saying my prayers!" She looked at him and replied, "You were saying your prayers, kneeling on the ground, facing east, with your head touching earth, praying to the Great Lord of the Universe, and you noticed that I fell over you? I was just chasing after my husband, whom I love dearly, and so didn't notice you, but if you said your prayers better, you'd be more attentive to the Lord of the Universe and not notice when someone falls over you."

The emperor listened to her words and was rather embarrassed. In fact, he honored her with gifts and sent her home to her beloved husband. And later, whenever the emperor prayed, he was not concerned with anything but Allah, blessed be the most Compassionate One, and whenever anyone asked him how he had learned to pray, he told them that a simple peasant woman who loved her husband had taught him to love the Lord of the Universe and what prayer really was.

This tale is delightful, enchanting and disarming, but as we talk about it, it seems to deepen and take on levels of meaning that are hidden within the text underneath the simplicity of the story and the relationships described. It is hard for any of us to admit that perhaps we don't know how to pray, especially if we've been doing it for a long time. But if we are not single-hearted, passionate and devoted about something or someone, then we will not know how to be that way with God.

We are touched by the emperor's simple devotion and obedience to the call to pray publicly, ritually, daily. We note that perhaps that kind of praying, as distracted as it appears to be, opens him to the honesty of the woman's insights and leads him to another kind of intensity and prayer.

We see in the story the interaction of doing justice in the world and praying. We often separate the work of caring for our brothers and sisters in action, in legal work, community organizing, from prayer, when the world drops away and we seek to enter a very sophisticated relationship between God and ourselves, alone in the world. It is as though we have two lives that run parallel. We pray as though God is intensely interested in us alone. We have to learn to bring the rest of the world into our prayer. Praying for someone else is hard, even praying for someone we love. It's even harder to pray for people who are difficult or annoying or who harm us and do us wrong. And then there are the people we never think to pray for or to remember. We forget so many, even in our prayer, which is the act of remembering ourselves and others before God. Whom do we forget to include or gather into our spirits and souls?

What does the story say about prayer? First, we need some passion in it. When the woman is confronted by the emperor she does not defend herself. She knows she was doing something important by looking for her husband, but she also knows the emperor was doing something important too, and she wants him to be sure to do it well.

If we do what we claim to be doing when we pray, there should be some sort of recognizable change in our relationships and behavior in the world as well as in the way we pray. Do we pray because it's rote, habit, what we are supposed to be doing? Do we pray the way our group thinks it should be done, or do we pray because God is God and we are not, and we claim to belong to this God, the Lord of the Universe, the Holy One, the Most Compassionate One? The woman sees the emperor as he really is and converts him to prayer, to what he might be before Allah. The emperor's prayer opens him to seeing and hearing himself and life from another's point of view and responding to that honestly and sincerely.

Prayer opens us to others' contexts rather than just absorbing others and sifting them through our contexts and using them to confirm or add to our already existing sense of self and life. If we really learn how to pray, to listen and to see, then we sit inside them, learning life from their hopes, weaknesses, strengths and questions. Then we respond to them in their world. Prayer allows us to sit inside God and see the world and history and our own small places in the universe from God's vantage point. It is a chance to see where God is coming from, as the woman sees where the emperor is coming from—the emperor is revealed in his prayer as incredibly self-centered, as most of us are. Prayer introduces us to being more concerned about God than we are about ourselves, to getting outside ourselves, to "denying our very self" internally and to opening up and out. In a sense, prayer is the process of being turned inside out so our souls and spirits, hearts and mind touch the world with vulnerability and passion and devotion as we do when we turn to face our God.

Parables are like this story, full of trap doors into another world, another vantage point, another focus, another insight into what we think we already know. It is an above ground world and a honeycomb of underground tunnels, and there are many entrances. Some we find; others find us! Here is the parable:

■ *Jesus told them a parable to show them that they should pray continually and not lose heart. He said, "In a certain town there was a judge who neither feared God nor people. In the same town was a widow who kept coming to him, saying: 'Defend my rights against my opponent.' For a time he refused, but finally he thought: 'Even though I neither fear God nor care about people, this widow bothers me so much I will see that she gets justice; then she will stop coming and wearing me out.'"*

And Jesus explained: "Listen to what the evil judge says" (Luke 18:1-6).

At first the parable fills us with confidence. If that evil, corrupt judge responds to a widow just to get her off his back, then what is God going to do for us? But then again, the judge is motivated only by fear and self-preservation. He only does what is right. How much more is God going to do for us? The comparison shows a gulf, a widening between how God will bring justice and how justice comes, finally, to those who cry out for it here on earth, to judges and structures and legal systems that oftentimes only respond because of fear, self-preservation and annoyance at those who are persistent in their need. But it takes so long, even here on earth. Is God going to wait before justice comes to earth? Is God going to wait for a long time to answer our prayers? Why does God not answer, not just a person's prayers, but the prayers and cries of the poor, of those who suffer innocently and unjustly in a world that cares little for justice. The psalms cry out repeatedly for God to rescue his people, to awake, to rise up and do justice, to stop hiding his face from his people and ignoring their miseries and woes, while others humble them to dust and smash their bodies to the ground (Psalm 44:23-

26). The prophets echo these pleas on behalf of those who have no voice, who are hoarse with crying out and not being heeded even by the religious and righteous of Israel. The book of Habakkuk begins:

> Yahweh, how long will I cry for help
> while you pay no attention to me?
> I denounce the oppression and you do not save.
> Why do you make me see injustice
> and wish me to look on tyranny?
> All I see is outrage and looting.
> The Law has been put aside
> and just decrees are no longer issued.
> The wicked overrule the upright
> and nothing is seen but crooked laws (Habakkuk 1:2-4).

Does the story say that the more we need and cry out for justice, the longer we have to wait for it? This parable comes immediately after Luke's account of the coming of the kingdom in its fullness and the warning that we don't know when justice and judgment and the end is coming. The last line of the preceding chapter is the disciples' question to Jesus: "Where will this take place, Lord?" Jesus answers, "Where the body is, there too will the vultures gather." The image is startling, even horrendous, and yet for those in need of justice, hopeful. When the day comes, those who cry out for justice will receive it as surely as those who did not do justice or hear the cry will be as corpses that vultures gather around.

After Jesus tells this parable of the widow and the unjust judge, he tells his disciples: "Will God not do justice for his chosen ones who cry to him day and night even if he delays in answering them? I tell you, he will speedily do them justice" (vv. 7-8a). When the justice comes, when the answer is given, when God responds, it will be thorough and strong and all encompassing. It will be swift justice, for his chosen ones.

And yet this is a parable about prayer. Sometimes we pray for years for something, and we don't get it. The standard answer to that is that God said no. People use this parable for hounding God, using the phrase, "the squeaky wheel gets the oil." We just have to persevere and eventually God will respond to us. This brings up issues of what we pray for, how we pray, whether we are praying correctly when we pray. When do we pray most fervently? When we're at the end of our ropes, when we're desperate, lonely, in despair, out of control, helpless, broken in spirit and body, when we are overwhelmed by sin, by our own and others' collusion with evil, or emptiness and rejection, when we are in need. When we get what we want, we are grateful and joyous. When we suffer and those we love suffer and we can do nothing, we pray and we pray when we remember who God is, in moments of loveliness and beauty in creation, in moments of the Spirit when incarnation creeps up on us and appears right in front of us.

When don't we pray? We fail in prayer when we have it made and are intent on our investments, objectives and work, when we're on a roll, when we're tired, when we despair and feel that God doesn't care.

This is a parable about praying always and continually and not losing heart. What is prayer? Is prayer words, presence, remembrance? God may be on our minds always, but we may lack the right intention. Or when we get older we may pray more because our life narrows down. Does opening to God mean we know God at all? In this parable the widow never gives up, never surrenders, never gives in, never quits. The judge does. But it is for all the wrong reasons that he decides to do justice. Many of us are more like the judge. We give in only after a long time and usually not for the best reasons in the world, either.

In the past this parable has always been interpreted with God as the Judge and us as the widow. There are insights to be gleaned from that image—comparison and opposition that God will come and do justice and it will be swift, not like the judge in the parable who cares neither for God's laws or the laws of people, just his own life and person. But in Chiapas, Mexico, I was sitting in on a group of people discussing this scripture and talking about praying when a woman stood up—which was unusual in the group—and said she had a speech to make. It was hard for her to do, but she wanted to say what she'd been thinking the whole time. What she said stunned me, stunned us all, and then it broke over us in a torrent of recognition and then later, like a tide returning again and again.

She spoke of being a widow, of going to a judge just like the one in the parable, and pleading for her rights: to find out why her son had been arrested and taken away, and where he was weeks after his disappearance. She hounded the judge day and night. She watched him, his moves, his daily schedule, his friends. She approached him every chance she had. She had nothing more to lose; she had already lost her husband, her other children. She was desperate. She grew to hate him, despise him and all those who were connected to the military, the jail, the courts. This had gone on so long. She prayed to God the same way while she pleaded and begged and got angry at the judge. And then as she listened to the parable she knew that she was the judge and God was the widow! We only get so persistent and long-suffering when we want something, not always or consistently. It is God who is always in our face, begging, pleading, cajoling, hounding us to do justice, to pray, to adore him alone and to respond as we should. God is the widow crying out for justice to us. We should be praying like that, like God who is always attentive and trying to get us to do justice, even if it is for the wrong reasons or for self-preservation or relief from God. God has nothing to lose; God has lost everything trying to call us back to repentance, forgiveness, justice, peace, mercy and living with one another as we should, obeying the laws of God and people. Of course! We all sat there, and some people started crying. God does not lose heart over us, over all the sin and evil in the world. God forgives again and again and calls us to do the same. We are the judge.

Just as we, often without thinking, make the widow an old woman, we see ourselves as the woman, the righteous one, the one demanding justice. We often pray like that, demanding our rights from God, when prayer is acknowledging we have no rights, that we rely on the mercy and justice of God and cast ourselves on his goodness, entrusting our hearts and lives to him alone. We put God in the role of the judge, who cares neither for the laws of God, covenant, reli-

gion or the land. We never think God might be the widow
and the tables might be turned. But why would Jesus tell a
story about prayer using his Father as a corrupt, uncaring,
insensitive judge, when he talks about his Father more in
the widow's terms: patient, faithful in spite of our responses,
loving, concerned, especially for the poor, the widow and
the orphan all through history? This is a parable about not
losing heart when we pray continually. Such prayer is a necessity of life, discipleship and work for justice and surviving in the world gracefully.

The story turns everything upside down. God is after us!
God is always after us, has been all through history, never
relenting, always finding new ways to catch us up. If the
judge is the type of those who are powerful and care neither
for God or human rules and laws, then God is the widow.
God is found in the powerless, those looking for justice. God
is on the side of the poor, those crying out for justice and not
getting it from us, from the systems and the structures of the
world, the church. If God is the widow, then God has a claim
on us. What is God's right? That we recognize our dependence on God alone. God is a widow woman with no viable
means of support in this world, except her rights. God is the
only God, a covenant God, and everything we do, own, know,
belongs to God. God calls us constantly to care for the least
among us if we are to be faithful to him. The prophets speak
on their behalf, and now God himself speaks on their behalf.
Prayer has a great deal to do with whether or not others are
getting justice and attention and dignity.

If Jesus calls his Father a widow, what is he saying about
God? Widows often are unemployable. They are oppressed
by laws; they are perceived as useless in society and culture;
they are not profitable; they are forgettable, lost. They aren't
supposed to get married again, but devote themselves to their
children. They are considered a burden to their families and
a problem in society. The widow is a nonentity. In Judaism a
widow had only one right under the law: if her husband had
a brother, he was required by law to marry the widow and
raise up children to her husband's name. Within the context
of Jewish society that was her protection. It gave her a place
in the family; it gave her security, a future and dignity. If her

husband did not have a brother, then she had no connections, no way to stay in the community. She became a beggar (like Naomi and Ruth in the Hebrew scriptures; two widows gleaning the fields and relying on a distant cousin to care for them).

But there is another small piece to the law according to some Jewish commentaries. If the woman did not have a brother-in-law to take her in and marry her, but had a son, the first-born son was required by law to care for her until he was thirty years old. This small piece of information is a catalyst for putting many pieces together: when Jesus brought the widow of Naim's son back to life, he saved two lives—the widowed mother's life as well as the son's. Jesus himself obeyed the law and cared for his widowed mother, Mary, for thirty years before taking on the public ministry of announcing the kingdom of the poor, of peace and justice. And Jesus gives his mother to young John, the disciple, so that she will be cared for in his community for years into the future. No wonder Jesus tells a story about his Father being a widow without rights. He was intimate with the situation himself, and the kingdom of heaven waited on a widow until the law was fulfilled.

Then who is the widow's opponent? Either her husband's brother, who won't marry her, or her own son, who won't take care of her. What if we are not the judge, but rather the opponent of the widow, related by blood or covenant and refusing to fulfill our obligations to our own sister-in-law or our own mother? If God is the widow and we are the sons and daughters of God, then we are the opponent in the story, the opponent who will not give God what is his by blood, by covenant, by law, by baptism.

Everyone is called to conversion in the parable, no matter who we think we are in the story or who God is. Whether we are the judge or the opponent, eventually God is going to get us, according to the story, and when he does he will bring swift, thorough and powerful justice in the name of the poor, the orphan, the widowed, the illegal alien, the stranger and foreigner in our midst. It's doubly hard to look at being the opponent because while there is a legal connection or relationship between the judge and the widow under the law of the land or the religious structure, the connection of the opponent with the widow is by covenant and blood, kin, and in our case, by baptism and Jesus' death and resurrection. Thus a much more sacred thing is defiled. We are the opponent in our personal relationship with God when we are the judge in our public relationship to the poor of the world. The two are two sides of the same coin. The one who searches for us, wakes us up, calls us to justice, to respond to the poor's rights is God—the widow, the poor who search us out. This reading of the parable makes God much more mysterious and powerful than the limited distinctions or description by opposition that the other interpretation must rely on. As someone once said: This is getting more and more awful to contemplate—what if the judge is not ruling in her favor because someone, the opponent is paying him not to? After all, corrupt judges are corrupt because they can be bought by the highest bidder. What if the opponents are paying off the system religiously or politically or economically so that they don't have to deal personally with the ones they are responsible for? Do we do that in our relationships with God and with one another?

Again—how to pray continually without losing heart? Jesus explains to the disciples: "Listen to what the evil judge says. Will God not do justice for his chosen ones who cry to him day and night even if he delays in answering them? I tell you, he will speedily do them justice. Yet, when the Son of Man comes, will he find faith on earth?" (Luke 18:6-8). What makes us lose heart? Individual experiences like depression, failure in relationships and the inability to change even when we want to. Other reasons: not to see results in work or prayer, or people who ignore us, refuse to acknowledge us, let alone encourage us in transformation of the world or ourselves. Isolation, selfishness, loss of self-esteem, statistics, the enormity of sin and evil, injustice in the world. The enormity of what we are up against, whether it is war, violence, AIDS, immigration, hunger.

What in the parable gives us hope? God doesn't lose heart! Beginning with creation God keeps coming up with creative, imaginative ways to respond to our destruction, our refusals, our ignorance and stubbornness and sin. God comes after us and will never stop, like the widow, until justice comes, until we know who we are, who God is, who our neighbor is, until we begin to do unto each other what we are called to do. It's wonderful news that God is after us! Jesus keeps saying this: that he has come to search out what is lost, to find and heal the broken-hearted, to bring good news to the poor. That is what Jesus is here for—unconditional love. God doesn't stop loving us no matter what we do or do not do. Instead, God devises more and more mysterious and humble and spirit-filled ways to get us to be human and love back. Unconditional love is not so much what we get on our end of the relationship, but the price and depth of what is given on the other end of the relationship and the length others will go to evoke love from those who keep refusing to accept it. God doesn't just love us no matter what we do, or in spite of what we do or don't do. Unconditional love says this: I will love you more when you do not respond. When you do evil I will absorb the pain and the destruction and come back again. If we accept that kind of unconditional love, like the widow's, then we must start living, loving, praying and struggling for justice the way God does, without losing heart.

Who's praying? We or God? Is God praying when we do? Is God "preying" on us? If we listen, respond and give God a chance to get us, maybe then, we learn a little about God. God is constantly praying for us. In Hebrew the word for prayer means to stand in the presence of God, to be seen for what we are, to be judged and not run away. It is the widow judging the judge, the widow judging the opponent and God, the widow and the poor judging us. There is prayer for comfort, for affirmation and confirmation, even praise, but this is prayer to see the truth, to be set free, to be converted, to do restitution, to obey and to be seen in relation to God and God's hearing always the cry of the poor, the widow, the least among us.

We pray in this parable to be what we claim to be as disciples and believers in Jesus, children of God. We pray to be confronted with the truth of the holiness of God and the justice that cries out to God and to us in our brothers and sisters. This kind of prayer is not to get something or to take something from God, but for God to take something from us and give it to whom it rightly belongs in justice. We know that God gets us when there is justice in the world, when the widow—and everyone—gets her right under God and in the community of Jesus. Justice and praying are equated in this story. When God gets us, we must respond like the judge and give what is called for. In the beginning, even if we only do it because of the judge's reasons, because we're afraid— well, that's a good enough place to begin.

The story hints that the judge is profiting from not ruling in her favor (perhaps by being paid by the widow's opponent). Are we, the children of God, in collusion with the unjust judge, the systems and dominant cultures and structures that keep justice from being done, that keep God's poor from being taken care of? God from the beginning has heard the cry of the poor, and someday God will bring justice to the earth and the poor. Some groups in South America and Mexico have said that if the only reason we begin to work for justice as the core of spirituality and liturgy is because we are afraid that God will do it, or the poor will rise up and do violence (as the New American Bible translates the reason for the judge's giving in to the widow), so be it.

Fear is the beginning of wisdom. If we are afraid that the widows and the poor and the aliens and the hungry will come after us someday—good. God is on their side and taking their part and hiding out as one of them, with them. When we do not do justice, we marginalize God in our life, robbing God of power. In a nutshell the story is saying that the less justice there is in the world, the less Jesus' disciples are praying. The more justice there is in the world, the more we are, in truth, hearing God and praying with heart. The emperor Akaba wasn't really praying according to the Hindu story, but the peasant woman taught him how to pray. The first person who teaches us to pray is the one who cries out for justice. When we hear that voice and respond, we realize that is God.

The last line of Jesus' explanation is the coup de grace: "Yet when the Son of Man comes, will he find faith on earth?" This line is full of pain, full of questioning, full of doubt, near despair because of the reality of the world, even among the disciples and those who claim to belong to the Son of Man, to Jesus, the Lamb of God, the Crucified One, the hope of the poor. When the Son of Man comes, will he find any faith on earth at all, among even his own people? We look at the parable as a condemnation of systems, structures, those in power, judges, and so on, and yet at the end Jesus turns it around on his own church, his own community, his own brothers and sisters, disciples—us.

The Son of Man will come, and he will judge, and the justice will be swift, sure and to the heart, like an arrow that tears through bone and flesh, like the double-edged sword of scripture. The judgment will be on the side of the poor, who had to wait long because we delayed in bringing that justice and care to those who deserved it. Jesus is talking to his own, to us. Why does it take so long for justice to come? Because we lose heart or don't pray or bring that justice though we claim to be the bringers of good news and a community that cares about the world. If we pray and don't change, then perhaps we are not praying. If we pray, we change, of necessity, and we are heartened. Justice will come one day, but every day we are being judged by the oppressed and those we ignore. Judgment is standing in the presence of God and letting God see us do something. In the words of Micah, only three things are necessary: to do justice, to love tenderly and to walk humbly with our God among the poor, the widow and the earth. God does not lose heart, so we are not allowed to lose heart either. We are bound to God by the waters of baptism, by friendship of the Spirit, by the blood of Jesus, the Lamb, the Son of Man, and by the voice and cry of the poor.

We are disheartened because we so often forget that God is with us, God is with the poor. It is the privileged place of revelation, of joy, of justice coming, of real faith on earth. Now is the time to pray, to cry out with the poor, to stand in the presence of God, the Son of Man and let God judge us, the poor judge us, the widow touch our hearts. It is time to stand fast with Jesus. It is time to fulfill God's hopes for us and know the heart of all that is made and human in the heart of God, who hounds us and has nothing else to do until forever.

After looking at the story in this way, we can begin to delve into the layers of meaning and associations that lead to conversion, individually and communally. We can seek to pray always and not lose heart. How? Do justice, endure, push our privilege, be tenacious, stand together with those who need a voice, accompany the poor, fulfill our responsibilities, oppose injustice, hope outrageously. This story says we are not allowed to despair! God is with us and will stand up against anyone or any structure. For now, God hides out and waits for the swift, fierce justice that follows the cross and resurrection.

7

The Talents

———— ■ ————

There are two versions of this parable, one found in Matthew (chapter 25), wedged in between the parable of the ten virgins with oil in their lamps and the parable of the sheep and the goats. This version is found in Luke (chapter 19), the last thing that Jesus tries to tell his disciples before he enters Jerusalem to face the cross and die. It is different from Matthew's story in that it adds historical background and is situated within Luke's chapters of how the kingdom comes and who is in it and who models discipleship in the practices of prayer, justice, economics, repentance and community. The parable is about talents—money. It is about economics, politics, power, authority and governments, not about talents that are personal and put to the use of the community. So, perhaps another story about money will get us thinking along the lines of the parable.

This is a story from the Middle Ages, from the Jewish community, and it bears traces of that community's interaction and life on the fringe of the Christian church. It is a parable, full of trap doors and quicksand to catch us off guard.

■ Once upon a time two men were born in the same village on the same day. One was born in the ghetto to a poor and struggling family, hungry all the time. All his life he wondered what it would be like to be rich. He was a good Jew, obedient to the law and even generous to beggars who were worse off than he was. He looked at the rich man's family, which lived on the hill above the town, and wondered what it would be like to have more than you needed, or lots of options, and he often was jealous of the life he was not given.

The other man was born to the rich family, and he lived with wealth, privilege and education. He too was a good Jew, obedient to the law, and generous to the poor and well respected in his community. He looked down on the village and the poor part of the town and saw all the poor people as pretty much the same, no one standing out at all.

And then, both men died on the same day. They got to the gates of heaven together and were very surprised to find St. Peter there waiting for them, with the gates wide open. He stepped forward and shoved the poor man aside and welcomed the rich man into the kingdom with open arms. In fact there was a red carpet rolled out, a band and trumpets, and all the kingdom of heaven turned out for a parade, speeches and a dinner in his honor.

The poor man was stunned and only managed to slip in before the gates closed unceremoniously. He watched in fascination, and he grew more and more concerned and angry. This is not the way it was supposed to be! He'd believed that because his life was hard on earth, he would be rewarded greatly in heaven, and that the rich on earth would have "hell to pay." But this was looking just like earth, with the rich being treated specially and the poor cast aside and forgotten. Why, nobody even knew he was here. He was in, but was it worth it?

He stayed around for the dinner and became even more angry and annoyed. It was a feast, a banquet, with glowing accounts of the rich man's life. Then came the last straw. The man was given keys to the biggest mansion the poor man had ever seen in his life—or his dreams. That was it! The poor man decided to tell Peter off and, if this was heaven, he wanted out. Hell couldn't be any worse than this. He boldly went up to Peter as things were winding down and accosted him loudly, reminding him that he was here too and that he was fed up. Peter was stunned and chagrined and apologetic, profusely welcoming him and telling him he was sorry that he had forgotten all about him. But the man would not be eased or mollified—he was indignant and wanted out. He listed all the things that the rich man had received and pointed out that he had gotten nothing—except the gates of heaven nearly slammed in his face. Peter tried to reassure him, telling him he did have a mansion, and it made the rich man's look like a shack. That slowed him down some, and he thought he'd go see it before he left in a huff.

He was taken deep into the kingdom, close to the throne of God. He couldn't believe his eyes—it was magnificent. Peter told him that the rich man's house was way outside the inner court of heaven. But the man was still angry—okay, so I have a really nice place close to the throne of God, but why didn't I get the red carpet and the fanfare and the music and the dinner and the speeches and the attention the rich man got—it wasn't fair. I know, said Peter, as he put his arm around the poor man, I know. But you have to understand. People like you come through here every day, but do you know how long it's been since someone like him got in?

The story is funny, and still it provokes much talk, even sobering discussion and anger and dissension. If we accept the story, we face some overwhelming conclusions and convictions and some hard decisions that can't be brushed aside easily.

Whose point of view do we take in the story? Usually we assume we are the one rich person who is going to make it into heaven, even though the story is adamant about how few and far between those folks are in reality. We may even get annoyed about the attitude of the poor man, who coveted the rich man's lifestyle, even in heaven. What it comes down to is: if this story is true, being poor or being rich has all to do with getting into the kingdom of heaven, but not just poverty and riches, but what is done with them on earth.

Being rich does not necessarily make it easier to be an observant religious person, generous with wealth, sensitive to others in life or dependent on God, just as being poor doesn't necessarily make it easier to be an observant religious person, generous with much less, sensitive to the sufferings of others or dependent on God or others. But the question arises: does being rich make it harder? Are riches a hindrance to everlasting life and care for the least of our brothers and sisters? Does being rich allow us to ignore the ultimate interdependence of humanity and the ultimate dependence on God alone?

Riches can isolate us and offer us so many options that it can be hard to commit ourselves to one thing, one group, one devotion, one path. Riches can allow us to buy our way out of many problems, legally and psychologically, for long periods of time, giving us the impression that we are not subject to the weaknesses of others. Wealth can make us feel superior or self-righteous or help us rationalize that we worked hard for what we have and deserve it, rather than seeing all as gift from the hand of a gracious God, who calls us to share all that we have with others and to bring ever more abundant life to others, especially those in need. Money can make us callous, intent on pleasure and amassing power and possessions. Like the rich young man in the gospel, we may be more attached to that independence and leisure and affluence than to a relationship with God as disciple, as a member of a community.

Let's look at money more specifically. What would we do if we received an unexpected $10,000? Most of us respond quickly with one or more of the following: bills, education, mortgage payments, vacations and cruises, hobbies; donations to the church, to missionary organizations, political groups, ecology groups; maybe contributions to the poor. But we think primarily of our pressing needs.

What if the government gave us the money? Would that change what you plan to do with it? For most, it wouldn't make any difference. Some may not trust the government, fearing it will take it back somewhere along the line, or tax it, or want an accounting, or that there may be some sort of hidden strings attached. If we are mistrustful, we may give it away quicker, perhaps to groups in need that aren't covered by tax-exempt status, like the Catholic Worker, soup kitchens, AIDS hospices or just families in need. Or we may just spend it freely.

Would we tithe? Most of us say "no way." A few would, some guiltily and some graciously, and a rare few might give it all away because of where it came from. Almost no one would refuse the money because the government gave it, questioning where the money came from, how the government got it, operating on suspicion of systems, and so on. Not accepting the money never enters most of our minds.

But what if we begin to consider that the government makes most of its money from taxes paid by middle income and lower classes of people, from arms sales to parties engaged in open hostilities and war, from laundering drug money, from investments in the World Bank, which charges exorbitant interest rates that adversely affect the poorer countries of the world? This becomes distressing and unsettling. Knowing where the money comes from and still using it becomes collusion with immorality and injustice. We are so steeped in the system that we never think to examine it, let alone stand apart from it or in opposition to it. We are so much a part of our economic and political reality, educated to its values and philosophies, that it never dawns on us that it might be luring us into a stance that is in conflict with the gospel of Jesus. We are children of our age, of capitalism, of rampant fiscal spending, of first-world misuse of resources and wealth. But somehow that is edited out of our consciousness when we listen to the gospel. And worse, we rationalize and interpret the gospel according to the existing systems of injustice without even noticing, until others who experience the system and class structures differently point out our blind spots.

We've looked at money and at systems. One more question will help prepare us for Luke's parable. What do we detest in a leader? The list is seemingly endless: dishonesty, hypocrisy, arrogance, patronizing behavior, deceit, using power and the law for personal gain, the use of violence,

racism, brutality, arbitrary decision-making, insensitivity to the suffering of others, deviousness, autocratic actions, pomposity, lack of sincerity, refusal to listen, indecisiveness, irresponsibility.
With this background, let's read the parable.

■ *Jesus was now near Jerusalem and the people with him thought that God's reign was about to appear. So as they were listening to him, Jesus went on to tell them a parable. He said, "A man of noble birth went to a distant place to have himself appointed king of his own people, after which he would return. Before he left, he summoned ten of his servants and gave them ten pounds (talents). He said: 'Put this money to work until I get back' (invest it). But his compatriots who disliked (hated) him sent a delegation after him with this message: 'We do not want this man to be our king.'*

He returned, however, appointed as king. At once he sent for the servants to whom he had given the money, to find out what profit each had made. The first came in and reported: 'Sir, your ten pounds have earned ten more.'

The master replied: 'Well done, my good servant. Since you have proved yourself capable in a small matter, I can trust you to take charge of ten cities.' The second reported: 'Sir, your investment earned five more pounds.' The master replied: 'All right, take charge of five cities.'

The third came in and said: 'Sir, here is your money which I hid for safekeeping. I was afraid of you, for you are an exacting (hard) person; you take up what you did not lay down and reap what you did not sow.'

The master replied: 'You worthless servant, I will judge you by your own words. So you knew I was an exacting person, taking up what I did not lay down and reaping what I did not sow! Why, then, did you not put my money on loan so that when I got back I could have collected it with interest?'

Then the master said to those standing by: 'Take from him what I have given and give it to the one with ten pounds.' They objected: 'But, sir, he already has ten!'

'I tell you: everyone who has will be given more; but from him who has not, even what he has will be taken away. As for my enemies who did not want me to be king, bring them in and execute them right here in my presence'" (Luke 19:11-27).

The story starts ordinarily enough. Someone in the government gives ten servants ten pounds each and tells them to invest it while he goes off to get himself crowned king in a foreign country. When he returns as king, he calls in his servants for an accounting. Simple enough. Ten servants, the same amount of money. Two of them really work at investing the money and come up with lots more—the first doubles it, the second earns five pounds more. Both are praised by the master and receive a reward for their stewardship—they get to take over ten cities and five cities respectively. The third one buries the money in the ground because he's afraid of the king—and with good reason considering what follows. But what happened to the other seven servants?

A parable begins as an ordinary event, in circumstances based on life experience that all share—a man becomes king even though a good number of his fellow citizens despise him and make it very clear publicly that they do not want him to be king over them. A typical case of political intrigue. But then the story turns ugly. He turns on the third man and judges him on his own words, his own character assessment. He takes the ten pounds from him and gives it to the one with ten already. Even the king's servants (those who are standing by) are appalled and object, but he's clear about his actions: the rich get richer and the poor lose what little they have and are excluded from the system. And then, his last act of judgment: all those who stood against him, opposed his kingship conferred on him by another country, are executed right there, without trial, without justice—an act of terrorism to wipe out any opposition and anyone who disagrees with him. Still, what about the other seven? Did they just disappear into the cities with the money or refuse to play according to his rules?

Jesus tells his disciples this story because they are close to Jerusalem, and they think the kingdom of heaven is about to make its appearance. They are keyed up, hopeful, expectant; they are not looking at reality, the reality of what is going to happen in Jerusalem. Jesus is telling his disciples to remember how the world operates. Those who don't play the games of power, politics, intrigue and injustice are going to get killed. Those who play the game but are afraid, will lose what little they have been given by the powers that be and the system. But those who play the game, will end up just like those who are in power, to varying degrees. Incidentally, the next line of the gospel is: "So Jesus spoke, and he went on ahead of them, on his way to Jerusalem" (v. 28). Jesus is going to be killed by such a king, Herod, who went off to Rome to get himself crowned by the occupying army and nation, who was detested and hated by his own people both for collaboration with Rome and for his brutality and lack of respect for the Jewish faith and people, his own people.

What does all this say theologically about us, about the way the kingdom comes into the world, about the world of politics and economics and governments everywhere in relation to the kingdom and the gospel of Jesus? If we are going to live a true Christian life in this world, we will be persecuted! If we follow the masters who rule in the world, we will end up just like them in values, actions and relationships and priorities, in money and power. But if we follow our master Jesus, we will end up in Jerusalem at the cross. We can't be both; we must choose. And the seven? Perhaps Jesus is saying that most of them will die eventually, along with him. The gospel is about risking crucifixion and believing in resurrection. It is about risking telling the truth, so that the kingdom of heaven might enter into this world through us. The world is based on power, violence, investments, interest (usury), exploitation, dominance, occupied territories, nationalism, arrogance, terrorism, slaying enemies without justice or recourse; it is about the rich getting richer and the poor becoming destitute and miserable by decisions made by those in power.

How did we get so off-base in our individualistic interpretations of this parable, stripping it of its basic element of economics, money and power in politics and nations? Why do we make God a harsh, vindictive despot, who slays his enemies and takes from those who live in fear of injustice and arbitrary power? Why do we insist on interpreting the parables and the stories so that they confirm existing conditions, endorse dominant cultural values, rather than convicting us of injustice, sin, evil or the need to be converted to the cross and community? The interpretation just presented is a radically different alternative to existing conditions, and some would say a subversive description of society. It affirms boldly that the kingdom of peace and justice, of dignity for all, of good news for the poor, comes in very different ways than the world says it does—and from the way many believers in Jesus think it does. The kingdom comes in conflict, in struggle, in the cross and suffering with others and, of course, resurrection. God stands behind Jesus and his disciples with power, but not the power of money, arrogance, dishonesty, hatred, violence and cold-blooded heartlessness.

The story is about power, and it is about money too. It says, many believe, that we must walk away from money, especially when that money comes from certain places and is used in ways that defy justice and the care of all in society with dignity. The gospel confronts us with what we claim to be, though we don't always put that claim into practice in history and geography and daily communal and personal life and choices. This parable is a warning. Jesus tries to prepare his disciples, who think the kingdom is coming soon. They think this because they are ignoring Jesus' words about the cross and rejection and persecution and death and because they are still marveling at the previous story about Zacchaeus and his total conversion. They have forgotten the incident of the young man, who is only one among myriads of those who chose not to change and to defy Jesus' call to the cross and denial of self and building up treasure in the kingdom by care of the poor.

We react strongly when we reflect on this story. We feel superficial, challenged, convicted, laid bare, angry. We sense the need for support, for people to stand behind us in a world that is sometimes, perhaps often, openly hostile to what Jesus asks of us. There is a certain amount of fear—fear of the Lord, which leads to wisdom; fear in the recognition that we might need to relent, repent and come home, having been on the wrong track, making the wrong choices, aligning ourselves with the wrong people. We fear evil and violence, and yet at the same time, we feel trust for Jesus goes ahead of us into Jerusalem. Even though he is the first to be slain in the presence of the kings, his kingdom is here, in the world, and we are trying to bring it more deeply into our lives and the lives of others.

So the story is also about hope, about good news. The kingdom is here in spite of the fact that many detest its presence and murder its followers and martyr the witnesses to its truth. It is the alternative to much of the experience of the world's people. Believers know that they do not want the kind of economics, politics, nationalism, terrorism, violence and disregard for people that is part of the world, and they know that the gospel offers alternatives of hope, a place of hospitality, the kingdom here and now for those who follow Jesus' way. It may be here only in small pockets and places, but it's here.

The parables are about how the kingdom comes in the context of violence, fear, injustice, amid nations and states, war and terror, and how it comes communally though based on personal choices. Our past readings of this parable reveal us to be so steeped in our own culture that, at best, we are first citizens and only then, perhaps, Christians, followers of Jesus. We are dominated by our lifestyles, individuality, nationalism, capitalism, personal incentive, and the need for security, profit, greed. We tolerate injustice and violence, and we rationalize it all, even using the gospel to further our culture's influence on us and others. But the parable tells us that the kingdom comes most clearly and powerfully in the death of anyone who stands against injustice and the kingdoms of this world that refuse to hear the good news of God. The parable asks us who and what we resist and where are we headed. What is really going on as the kingdom seeks to enter the world through believers? Whom do we travel with? Do we have a community that carries us as Jesus carried his disciples into Jerusalem and as Jesus carried his cross on behalf of others?

This parable questions us, examines us and asks us who we are. Do we play the game well and win high praise from society, shared power and good living? Do we play the game not quite so effectively, but still well enough to grab a share in the power in our small kingdoms? Do we react to systems and institutions like the third servant, saying we have trouble with this system and its ruler, but trying to hang on to what we've got? If so, eventually all we have is taken and given to those who have much already. Or are we one of the seven who disappear, fall through the cracks in the system, who don't seem to count at all. Are we perhaps among the compatriots of the king who don't want him as ruler and are executed within the context of the system's politics and violence? In Jesus' own community ten are executed, killed, one is exiled, and one commits suicide. The women mostly disappear, in religious structures as well as nations and countries.

And Zacchaeus, the one who sees Jesus, is converted, baptized and saved, who sits down to table with Jesus—Eucharist. What happened to him? He is remembered in the Christian community, but he disappears from the history of the world. He is now a disciple, a rich man who made the option for the poor and did justice and entered the church as a brother to Jesus. He obeyed the fundamental imperative of the gospel and Jesus rejoiced exceedingly at his dinner party!

Here is another story for remembering. It is from the Sufi tradition of the Muslims, a teaching story, still used today to keep before the minds and hearts of the disciples the necessity of facing reality and acknowledging what is entailed in being a disciple. A note: a murshid or a caliph is like a Jewish rabbi or teacher, and in Islamic law, when people are counted, men are counted as one and women are counted as a half. The name of this story is "One and a Half Followers."

■ Once upon a time a man became the head of the Ottoman Empire, the sultan of the desert, rich and powerful in his vast domain. Many of his advisors immediately began to warn him about this caliph who had hundreds of thousands of followers. They spoke of danger to the sultan: that if the caliph sided with his enemies he could overthrow the sultan and rule in his stead, or he could organize his own followers and revolt. But the sultan ignored them and went about the business of running his kingdom.

Years passed and there were uprisings and coup attempts and tries at assassination and the name of this one caliph kept coming up. Finally the sultan decided to act on their accusations, and he summoned the man from the desert. He met him alone, at the edge of the desert and the man came, on his great steed, dismounted and knelt with his head on the ground. He then arose and said the ancient oath of fealty: "You, sir, are my master. Whatever power I have in the desert, you shared yours with me. Whatever knowledge and wisdom I have in the desert, you taught me. I will gladly give my life that my master may live." He said this with his hand over his heart, solemnly and before Allah.

The sultan embraced him and looked at him with delight and exclaimed: "I've wondered how you are, my friend. Do you know that my advisors are always warning me about you, the man with the hundreds of thousands of disciples? They do not know that you were once my disciple and still are, and so all of your disciples are mine." They talked of the good old days in the desert and the times of closeness and struggle.

Toward the end of the day the sultan asked him: just between you and me, how many followers do you have? The caliph pondered the question and finally said one and a half. The sultan reacted angrily and said, "Who do you think I am? Why would my advisors warn me about someone with one and a half followers? Well, we'll find out just how many you do have."

The sultan ordered his soldiers to arrest the caliph, and threw him into a dungeon. He sent a message throughout the desert saying that their master, the caliph, had fallen from grace with the sultan, and that if they didn't all show up on a certain day he would be beheaded. Unbeknown to anyone else, he had a tent set up on the edge of the desert and had thirty sheep put into it and a dozen of his best soldiers. And he waited for the day to come.

The caliph was dragged from his underground prison, and he and the sultan waited at the edge of the desert, the caliph in chains beside his old master. And they came by the thousands before dawn, on camel, horseback, ass and donkey and on foot until as far as the eye could see there were men, women and children. The sultan turned to the caliph and said: "One and a half followers. Who the hell are all these people?" The caliph said nothing. Then in the silence as the sun rose, the sultan stepped forward and spoke loudly. "This man, your master, has fallen from grace. If ten of you are willing to give your life so that your master might live, then step forward. Otherwise I will behead him now." And he drew his sword.

There was a terrible silence. People started sweating, and finally one man stepped forward and put his hand on his heart and said the ancient oath: "Sultan, this man is my master. Whatever power I have in the desert, he shared his with me, and whatever knowledge and wisdom I have in the desert he taught me. I will gladly give my life so that my master might live." The sultan snapped his fingers and the soldiers marched him up to the tent, took him inside, dropped the flaps. They slit the throat of three sheep and the blood began to seep down through the sand.

There was a murmur in the crowd and some started slipping back into the desert. Not a lot, but enough so that you'd notice. The silence and the heat stretched. Finally the sultan spoke again. "That's only one. I need nine more, or your caliph dies." Again the silence deepened, and the tension became terrible. Finally, a woman stepped forward, and even the sultan groaned outwardly. She put her hand over her heart and spoke the oath: "Sir, this man is my master. Whatever power I have in the desert, this man shared his with me. Whatever knowledge and wisdom I have in the desert, this man taught me. I will gladly give my life so that my master might live."

The sultan snapped his fingers again, the soldiers marched her up to the tent and took her inside. They slit the throats of three more sheep, and the blood started to gush down on the sands. And the crowd panicked and all bedlam broke loose. They ran back into the desert the way they had come. By sundown no one was left as far as the eye could see, only the sultan and the caliph in chains.

The sultan bent and set his friend free, and lifted him up, apologized and said: "I'm sorry. You were right. You only have one and a half disciples. You must feel terrible. All this time and work and that's all you have." The caliph stood and looked at his old master and said: "Sultan,

I know what you are thinking. You are thinking that the man is my one follower and the woman is the half." "Of course," the sultan replied. "Well, you're wrong," the caliph said. "The woman is my one follower and the man— he is arrogant and naive, but he has possibilities. He's my half."

The sultan sputtered and said: "But the law . . . " and he couldn't finish. The caliph said: "Sultan, discipleship has nothing to do with the law; it has to do with love and devotion. Let me explain. When the man stepped forward he didn't know he was going to die. He thinks everything is a test. He has a lot to learn. But when the woman stepped forward, she knew she was going to die. She is my one follower." And the sultan was quiet.

When they tell this story today they ask: "Which one are you? Are you the man who is arrogant and naive and thinks everything is a test but has some possibilities? Or are you the woman who knows that if you follow a master you will die? Or are you one of the hundreds of thousands who just *think* you are somebody's follower?"

It was Dietrich Bonhoeffer who said: "When Jesus bids us come and follow him, he bids us come and die. The question is: what do we die for, whom do we die with, and whether or not we come after Jesus into Jerusalem."

8

The Lost Son

———— ■ ————

The story of the prodigal son is probably one of the best loved and most often told stories of Jesus. It is found in chapter 15 of Luke, the third part of the stories of the lost sheep, the lost coin and the lost son. All the stories are fantastic, unbelievable. Who would leave ninety-nine sheep behind to be preyed upon by wolves, dogs, thieves, and go after the one that wanders off by itself? Or a woman who loses one coin from her dowry, would she really light a lamp, sweep the house and do a thorough search, and then call all her neighbors to rejoice with her over finding the one piece she lost? Who would really care? Yet we are told that there is rejoicing in the same manner among the angels of God over one repentant sinner. Either there aren't too many repentant sinners or the angels really know how to throw a party and rejoice! And then we come to the longest of the three stories, often called the parable of the prodigal son.

All three stories are told in the context of Jesus sitting around with tax collectors and sinners, all of them eager to hear what he has to say. But the scribes and Pharisees are frowning and muttering: "This man welcomes sinners and eats with them." So Jesus tells them these stories. They are directed at the "acceptable" ones of religion and society: scribes, Pharisees, ministers, good religious people. This parable is hard to deal with because so many people are so attached to it, heavily invested in it because of their image of God—the prodigal's father and the story of repentance, mercy and rejoicing—often used as the basis of first penance and confession and communal services.

Perhaps an old Jewish story that is told in Orthodox Jewish and also in Muslim groups (because the main character is Moses) will help prepare us for the over-turning of reality and rude awakening of this parable. There are many such stories about Moses, in which he still roams the world, still goes up the mountain to see God, still prays on behalf of the people and still comes down the mountain to tell the people what they need to remember and put into practice. Moses is still the leader of the people and the prophet and the giver of the law, the liberator.

■ Once upon a time, Moses was heading up the mountain to see God, as he did, and he decided to take a different route through a small town he didn't visit often. Just as he got inside the town limits he saw a Jew coming out of the synagogue. The Jew looked at him and thought he recognized him! "Moses," he asked, "is that you?" "Yes," Moses said. "Are you going up the mountain to see God?" "Yes," Moses replied. "Uh, Moses, would you be willing to do me a favor and ask God a question for me?" "Sure," said Moses, "what can I do for you?" "Well," the man said, "could you ask God if he ever thinks about me, and would you remember me to him?" "Sure," said Moses, and went on toward the mountain.

When he was almost all the way through the town he was recognized again—this time by a bum leaning up against the wall of a building. He perked right up and said: "Moses, is that you?" Moses reluctantly answered that it was. "Moses," he said, "are you going up the mountain to see God?" Moses again said, "Yes." "Uh, Moses," he asked, "would you be willing to do me a favor and ask God if he thinks of me and remember me to him?" "Sure," said Moses, shaking his head. And off he went up the mountain to see God.

Moses spoke with God and listened to the words he was to bring to the people, and he almost forgot to mention the two men he had met on his journey. "Oh, God," he said at the last, "I met this Jew coming out of the synagogue, and he asked me if I'd remember him to you and ask you if you ever think of him." "Oh, yes," God said, "you tell him I see him often and think of him often and that I have reserved one of the best seats in the kingdom of God for him." "All right," said Moses. "And the other man, the bum leaning up against the side of the wall, he asked to be remembered too and wondered if you ever think about him?" "Oh yes," God said, "you tell him I think of him often, though I don't see too much of him, and that I have a seat reserved for him in one of the lowest parts of hell." "All right," said Moses. And off he went, back down the mountain and through the town.

It had been three days, but the bum was still leaning up against the wall and immediately saw Moses coming. "Moses, did you see God?" "Yes," Moses said. "Well, did you ask him about me?" "Yes, I did, and he said to tell you that he thinks of you often and knows you well but he doesn't see you too often and that he has a seat reserved for you in one of the lowest areas of hell." And much to Moses' surprise the man threw his arms around him, pounded him on the back and danced up and down for joy—"God remembers me, God thinks of me and knows me. Moses, you have made my day, in fact you've made my whole life!" And Moses left him still dancing up and down deliriously. Moses shook his head, wondering about the man.

On the way through town he saw the good Jew coming out of the synagogue again. The Jew ran over to him immediately. "Moses, did you see God?" "Yes," was Moses' answer. "Well, did you ask him about me?" "Yes, I did, and God says to tell you that he thinks about you often, sees a good deal of you and knows you well and that he has reserved a seat for you in one of the highest areas of heaven." The man was elated. He jumped up and down, threw his arms around Moses and was delighted and ecstatic. "Oh, Moses, you've made my day, you've made my whole life. All this has meaning, all this prayer, and God is true and wonderful. Thank you." And Moses went his way.

Well, the years passed and Moses took different routes to the mountain. Then one year as he was headed back up the mountain he walked through the same town. He heard that both men had died that year, and he made a note to himself to ask God where they were and how they each were doing. God and Moses talked, as they always did, and right before Moses got ready to leave, he casually asked God if he remembered those two men that he had talked about years before. "Yes, Moses, I remember them. What do you want to know?" "Uh, how are they?" "You really mean, where are they, Moses." "Yes," he replied. "Well, Moses, the bum leaning up against the wall is sitting next to me in the kingdom of heaven, and the good Jew coming out of the synagogue is sitting in one of the lower rims of hell." Moses was stunned and horrified. He thought to himself: God lied to me. God, knowing Moses, being God, said to him, "Moses, you forget. I am God, and I don't lie." Moses stuttered and said, "But, Lord, you said they had seats in opposite places." "No, Moses, I said they had reserved places in hell and heaven, respectively." "I, I don't understand," said Moses.

"Moses, when you told the bum that I knew him, what did he do?" "Oh," he said, "he acted very strangely, dancing up and down for joy. I thought he was crazy, deranged." "But Moses," God said, "he was rejoicing that I, God, thought of him, remembered him, who is nothing, and that day he began to climb into the kingdom of heaven." Then Moses said, "But the other man, the good Jew reacted the same way, dancing up and down and singing your praises." "No, Moses," said God, "he was delighted and relieved not that I remembered him but that all this had meaning and that what he was doing and his praying was having an effect. That day he started sliding into hell."

"Oh," said Moses, thinking. And Moses turned to go back down the mountain. As he left, God called out to Moses, "Moses, just because you spend a lot of time with me doesn't mean you know me at all." And Moses descended the mountain wondering, for the first time in his life, whether he would end up in heaven or hell.

If Jesus had told this story to the scribes and the Pharisees, what would they have thought?! Would they have wondered if they had the best seats in the house after all? Would they have put themselves in Moses' place, wondering if they truly knew God, even after spending so much time with him? Do we put ourselves in that vulnerable position? The story casts doubt over a lot of our choices, in the past as well as the present. It puts us in the frying pan, and the heat's on! It makes us question God's criteria for holiness, for entrance into the kingdom. It shatters any thought that we can earn our way into the kingdom, or that we deserve it. It says to obviously religious people: be careful. Because we are heavily invested in religion doesn't say we know anything about God. It says that perhaps the bum up against the wall is truer in his heart than the one person in church. Outward manifestations are not always good indicators of what is going on inside. Be careful of good religious appearances, they may be doing more for us than for God or our neighbors. The bum knows that he needs God, that God is God. He is amazed that God even thinks of him, let alone keeps him in mind.

The parable is disconcerting. It's not just about the religious Jew and the bum; it is more about Moses, the leader, the speaker, the one who perceives himself as having a privileged relationship with God, like the scribes and the Pharisees, like most of us in church.

Now we turn to the parable Jesus told to the religious community and those excluded and cast out from them for their behavior or connections.

■ *"There was a man with two sons. The younger said to his father: 'Give me my share of the estate.' So the father divided his property between his two sons.*

Some days later, the younger son gathered all his belongings and started off for a distant land where he squandered his wealth in loose living. Having spent everything, he was hard pressed when a severe famine broke out in that land. So he hired himself out to a well-to-do citizen of that place and was sent to work on a pig farm. So famished was he that he longed to fill his stomach even with pig's food, but no one offered him anything.

Finally coming to his senses, he said: 'How many of my father's hired men have food to spare, and here I am starving to death! I will go back to my father and say to him: Father, I have sinned against God and before you. I no longer deserve to be called your son. Treat me then as one of your hired servants.' With that thought in mind he set off for his father's house.

He was still a long way off when his father caught sight of him. His father was so deeply moved with compassion that he ran out to meet him, threw his arms around his neck and kissed him. The son said: 'Father, I have sinned against God and before you. I no longer deserve to be called your son. . .'

But the father turned to his servants: 'Quick! Bring out the finest robe and put it on him. Put a ring on his finger and sandals on his feet. Take the fattened calf and kill it. We shall celebrate and have a feast, for this son of mine was dead and has come back to life. He was lost and is found.' And the celebration began.

Meanwhile, the elder son who had been working in the fields was now on his way home. As he neared the house he heard the sound of music and dancing. He called one of the servants and asked what it was all about. The servant answered: 'Your brother has come home safe and sound, and your father is so happy about it that he has ordered this celebration and killed the fattened calf.'

The elder son became angry and refused to go in. His father came out and pleaded with him. The indignant son said: 'Look, I have slaved for you for all these years. Never have I disobeyed your orders. Yet you have never given me even a young goat to celebrate with my friends. Then when this son of yours returns after squandering your property with loose women, you kill the fattened calf for him.'

The father said: 'My son, you are always with me, and everything I have is yours. But this brother of yours was dead, and has come back to life. He was lost and is found. And for that we had to celebrate and rejoice'" (Luke 15:11-32).

The story fills us with admiration for the father. We also feel humbled, grateful, sorry, sad, indignant, resentful. The parable subverts our reality and feelings. And each time we hear the story, it tries to move us somewhere else, hopefully nearer to the kingdom. The parable is like a doorway into the kingdom. We find ourselves in another world—the kingdom of God. And Jesus is the parable of God.

What do we feel as we hear this story? We are indignant at the property owner who sends the young man off to the pigs and doesn't do anything to help him or relieve his hunger. We resent the younger brother because of his behavior, but also because, according to Jewish law, the father gave away the elder son's inheritance, breaking the law. The elder son was to inherit it all and then decide how to divide it. In exchange for this privilege, it was also his responsibility to act as reconciler and go-between for the father and the children. This is a very strange father who creates dissension in his own family by giving away the older son's portion, and then, when the younger one comes home, he gives him still more! No wonder the older brother is resentful of the father's actions and love for the younger son. We are annoyed with the younger brother, who comes home only because he's hungry. Some repentance! He's still using the father. And we have trouble with a father who is so foolish, accepting the wayward son back, throwing a big party for him and creating more dissension in the family. The forgiveness shown by the father is incredible, beyond anything rational or expected. We are amazed by it.

Who is in the story, and what can we learn about them? First, there is the servant who tells the brother out on the land that his brother is home. Servants know everything that's going on in a family, in a household. He knows that the older son will not be happy at all with this development. The servant knows what this father and both brothers are like.

The people to whom the story is told are scribes and Pharisees, good Jewish religious people who would never think of hanging out with the people that Jesus is with, let alone eat with them. And yet the story is about a feast, a meal of rejoicing, of eucharistic community with tax collectors and the prostitutes and sinners. There are two groups here: good religious people who know the law, follow the law and know when others don't. They are the leaders, the norm in the community, the teachers. They are looked to so that others know what to do and how to live. The scribes are educated in the law and religion, paid professional ministers in the employ of the Pharisees, using their knowledge for those who pay for it. Both scribes and Pharisees have power and control; they are elders in the society.

What of the others—the tax collectors, prostitutes and sinners, people who publicly sin or do evil as a way of life? Today who would they be? To answer that question is risky, because we are judging others and putting them in groups. We know that everyone is a sinner but there are two groups of sinners: public and private, those who are known by their sin and those who are not known by their sinfulness. Everyone falls from grace, but a lot of religious people or church people act as though they don't. Tax collectors were Jews who were appointed by the Romans to collect taxes from their neighbors. Only the Romans and the collector knew what was due, so anything the tax collector collected over and above was his. Tax collectors were detested and despised because they lived in collusion with the Romans who occupied the territory and because they lived well off their neighbors' labor and money. Today they would be bankers, with their interest charges, beggaring people to keep a lifestyle active. Prostitutes were not just sexual partners for hire. All other religions engaged in temple prostitution, so they were seen as betraying the Jewish covenant as well as breaking the laws of marriage, society and sexuality.

Other public sinners at the time of Jesus were those who sold their inheritance, pig keepers, shepherds, those who raised pigeons, those who left the covenant, Samaritans and more. Note the behavior of the younger son. He starts out by betraying his father, selling his inheritance and squandering it in licentious living and then is reduced to taking care of the pigs. The younger son is definitely in the public sinner category in the story and reality. He broke faith with his father, with his religion, with the Jewish people and with God. He sells a piece of the promised land—rejecting everything and so is rejected completely by the Jewish nation. He has gone as far down as he can. If he comes back, he knows he has to face the crowd, the mob, insults, stoning, perhaps even death for his behavior and betrayal.

Today public sinners are those who pay on a regular basis for what they have done or who they are and where they find themselves. Some people say the poor are in that category, as are prisoners or anyone who has been in jail, AIDS victims, the unemployed, the homeless and beggars, the races that are not dominant in any culture, drug addicts, homosexuals, the handicapped, drunks. Prostitutes are still in that group, and so are those who live together and are not married and single-parent families. There are many others. At the time of Jesus the worst thing Jews could do was give up their religion and take with them part of the communal inheritance, the promise of faithfulness, the land of the people. That is the younger son in the story. The scribes and Pharisees would have been horrified to see how the younger son fares. It is unthinkable. This younger son tells his father he wants him dead and turns to a life of licentious, irresponsible behavior. He becomes hated by his older brother. He is demanding, selfish, cold-blooded, only looking out for himself, being individualistic and rejecting his people, his family, his religion. He wants a little excitement in life, adventure; his family is boring. Yet he doesn't eat the slops; his Jewishness is still operating somewhere in there. But he thinks he can go home and get himself hired onto his father's estate and get paid and eat well—self-preservation is big with him. He's going back on his own terms.

So he goes home. And his father sees him coming from a long way off—he's out looking for him daily. In a Jewish community the houses were in the very center. The market place and other buildings were around them and then the open fields. Every day the father has gone out, waiting for his son to return, knowing that if he does, he will accompany him back and save him from the insults, stones and garbage that would be thrown at him. The father humiliates himself daily in front of his family, friends, villagers, even strangers. He has no other life but to bring his lost son home. So he runs out to him. The son tries to get out his prepared speech, but his father's arms are around his neck, hugging and kissing him, cutting out the words. The father doesn't care *why* he came back, just *that* he came back. And he orders the servants to bring out the ring, the robe and the sandals.

He tells him with these gifts that he never left, he is back as son in the family. Then the feast begins.

If the story stopped there, what would Jesus be saying? The story is about a father who does some very strange things. He's stupid in our terms, letting himself be used. But the story is loaded in the first line: a man had two sons, just like the two groups listening to the story, one getting it pointed directly at them and the others listening in. One is a public sinner, and the other is a private sinner, both sinners through and through. The first half is about the younger son and the public sinner, and the second half is about the elder son and the private sinner. Both need to deal with the father. This father breaks the law of Jewish tradition in giving the younger one his inheritance. It was unheard of that any father or head of the household would give it away before he died! And when the son comes back he is reinstated into the family, even though he has lost a good part of the estate. He will get another third, at least, out of what is left. Some exegetes even say that the ring means he got it all. In effect he was made the first son, the elder, by the father's actions. In breaking the law the father sets up a dichotomy between his children.

The father gave his children freedom. He allowed them to do what they wanted, even wanting him dead and out of his life, as in the case of the younger son, or refusing to come in, like the elder one. Whatever they do doesn't seem to have any effect on what the father does. He goes out to both.

After going out every single day since the younger son left, now the father has to humiliate himself again, leave the party, his neighbors and younger son, and go out to the other one, plead in the field and try to drag the other in. The other son left, but the older son has never really been there—he's been waiting for his father to die, thinking of himself as a servant, slaving for his father, resentful and selfish and angry.

We may get very annoyed with the father, letting both sons get away with what they do, treating him so callously, each in their own way. There is no sense of justice in the whole story. The father is too passive; he lets his children control him. He lives only for his children and having his family together. He needs some assertiveness training. He sets up conflict and copes with it through love, generosity, graciousness—not like us at all.

We most often go the route of the older son: ignore the father, refuse to be a part of the celebration, pout, get angry, throw what his father does in his face, fear the father. He certainly isn't obeying his father right now. He's humiliating him and pushing him away, blaming him, angry. He doesn't know his father at all. All he thinks about is himself and his friends. The brothers are really not so different. But he stays at home, watching over what's left of his inheritance. We can understand this son's reaction, and we want to excuse him. The father is clearly hard to live with.

But everyone has to change, younger or elder. If we are the younger son, we are ostracized from the community. The younger son lost his self-respect, dignity and self-identity. He knows that his brother hates him and refuses to come in, talk to him or even see him. He must wonder what everybody else in the community is thinking about him. He knows he is going to pay for a long time for what he's done, because the memory of the community, fueled by his brother, is going to be long.

The elder brother is a sinner too, but in a more private and secret way. The only difference between the two brothers is that the elder son assesses his own behavior positively and forgets what he himself has done wrong. He dissociates himself from his brother, calling him "that son of yours." He's left the family too. The younger brother is closer to the kingdom than he is. He's been in the family, close to the father all this time, longer because he is older, and yet he has no sense of the father's love, the father's intentions and desires. He shares none of his father's feelings or dreams and cares nothing for him. As an older brother he was responsible for his younger brother. It was his responsibility to go after his younger brother and not let something like this happen, not let his father be humiliated in front of his neighbors and compatriots. At least he could have gone out daily to see if he was returning.

Jesus is telling this story as if he is the older brother of the sinners, and he has gone out after them all, and now he's trying to get them to act like older brothers and sisters are supposed to act in the family of God. He lives for no other reason than to go out after us—our Good Shepherd. Jesus is our older brother, and we are the children of God. This brother in the story is in opposition to the father and to Jesus, because he has never done what the father wants—taking care of one another and going after the ones who have strayed, celebrating their return and starting all over again and, at all costs, holding the family together. The covenant of the Jews was about this, and Jesus' covenant is the same and we must celebrate. We have been with Jesus and the Father all this time, and we never think to go out after the lost. We too often stay because of what we get out of it, even in church, and still we have no understanding of who the father is.

The story ends with a play on words: "This son of mine that was lost is found, now he is alive!" When he leaves the older son in the field, his last words to him are, "This brother of yours was dead and has come back to life; he was lost and now is found." If we continue with the unspoken analogy it is, "Now you are dead and lost, unless you come in." That is the undercurrent of the parable, and the scribes and the Pharisees know that and hear it clearly. To refuse to associate yourself with brothers and sisters who have sinned in the family is to put yourself outside, is to sever the relationship. So the father will send his only son to them too—Jesus.

The story ends there, with the father going back to the celebration, leaving the elder brother to decide. The invitation to intimacy is still there, the invitation to learn to become an older brother and sister as Jesus is to us and to become that for others in gratitude. The longer we are in the church, the more we are looked at as the older brothers and sisters of Jesus and children of God. How are we doing? Are we going to be judged on what we have done for sinners, whom we have gone after, who has wronged us, and whether or not we sit down at table with them in Eucharist? How we relate to those who have taken what we thought rightfully belonged to us, whom we have shared with, whom we have been called to be responsible for, those who have made our lives hard and revealed who we are to God—these will all factor into our being with the father, like the elder brother in the field.

If we are the older children of God, what is given to us is given for the community, for the least, the weak, the youngest, the newest. We are responsible for keeping them at home, in relation to the father and connected to us. It is all about forgiveness and the way into the kingdom. The younger son gets it, and the older is offered it, but if we take it, we must return the favor of the father. We say it in Jesus' prayer daily: Forgive us our debts as we forgive those who are in debt to us, who owe us. We are given it because God cares that we are all held together as one family. All we must do is pass it on.

Part of it is just waiting, as the father waits for his children to be together again, for whatever reason—even one of them just coming to his senses and figuring out how to get back. But when the opportunity presents itself, the father moves and acts passionately. He has a long-range vision of what can be, in spite of what others feel, and he waits attentively and moves quickly so that others cannot do harm to those who return for whatever reasons. And then we get everyone involved in the celebration and, lastly, we leave the celebration and go after the ones that don't want to be involved but have been in the family forever. It's harder to deal with the people who are with us all the time, who think that they are not all that bad, that the problem is with others, never them, never us.

In the end one son comes in, but we just don't know about the other. Does he come in? All the parables call us to radical, drastic change in our life, like the younger boy who had to come home. He really had no other choice; he was desperate and at the end of his rope. The older son thinks of himself as a slave, is angry, a son who does not love his father or his brother. He is told that his brother is found, his brother is alive.

Jesus is killed for his storytelling. Every time they heard a story, those in power were more and more convinced that Jesus was going against the law, the covenant, destroying the community and the accepted understanding of justice, God and what constituted being a Jew. The parables don't end happily ever after; they bring us to the edge of a cliff. To make the story end, we have to jump, not knowing what is at the bottom of the cliff except what Jesus says in his story.

Here he confronts us with the question: if we are the elder son or daughter, then what do we have to do in order to come in to the feast, Eucharist, the kingdom of God? Depending on how long we have been the elder child, what is it going to take to change our relationship to the Father and to our younger brothers and sisters, all sinners in the family—or are we just going to up and come in? All the gospels tell us, all the stories say repent, relent. But it doesn't dawn on us that the closer we are to God the more responsible we are for others, that knowledge and intimacy with God brings responsibility.

If we call God our Father, then the way we know we are the children is the way we care for one another, especially the straying, the lost, the public sinners, the desperate and the ones we couldn't care less about, generally speaking. Jesus is trying to tell good religious people that the more we get comfortable in our religion and beliefs, the greater the possibility that we don't know God at all. Sometimes the ones who come back—no matter what the reason—have more of a sense of the father's graciousness, divine mercy and unfathomable love and tender regard for all his children, who sin and pain him and humiliate him daily.

The story is about the lost son, who perhaps stays lost, chooses to stay lost, even though God's mercy comes looking for him again and again. Jesus preaches unconditional love of the Father, the love that will do anything, including humiliating himself. In Jesus, this love allows others to kill him, still proclaiming forgiveness and love, so that we can see who we are and begin to practice that same unconditional love and do whatever it takes to get others to return home because of the graciousness that has been extended to us.

We need to pass on the gifts of mercy, forgiveness and unconditional love that we accept from God, giving them to another who needs them as desperately as we needed them. Jesus is trying to reveal to us, all of us, our own sinfulness, because some try to lay blame only on others and not accept it as common to all. Jesus is saying that the mercy extended to one, anyone, is salvation for all and will be extended to all. Some take it and some don't; some take it but don't pass it on.

The story invites us to come in and celebrate someone else's acceptance of mercy. Then perhaps we will be able to accept the mercy too. We are all in this together as the children of God. There are others getting in before us—public sinners with whom we won't sit down and eat. They're already eating with Jesus, sharing bread, Eucharist, and in the midst of the party he may have to come out and see if he can plead on his Father's behalf for us to come in. He will be acutely conscious of who is not there. We want Jesus, but we don't want them. And Jesus says we can't get him without taking them to heart too. There is a saying among storytellers that the story begins when the teller stops talking. It begins now—a story of hope.

Here is an old Jewish story from as many as six centuries before Jesus. It too is about two brothers and their father.

■ Once upon a time there was an old man who had two sons, and the time came for him to die. He called his sons together and told them he was handing on his land to them. To the older son, who had been with him longer and knew him better, he gave the harder land, because he would know how to work it. To the younger son he gave the bottom land, the best land, because he hadn't been with the father as long and did not know how to farm as well. And then he told them to remember that they were his sons, his children, and brothers always, and always to stay together in heart even if they were separated in life and circumstances. Soon after he died, and the two sons took their land and began their lives.

The older son never married. He worked the poorer land, but did very well on it. The younger son married and had many children. He worked the bottom land and sometimes did well, but he needed everything to care for and feed his family. Many years went by, and the brothers did not see each other, so involved were they with their separate lives.

One night late the older son was counting wheat sheaves in his barn and wondered how his younger brother was doing. He thought: My younger brother has so many mouths to feed that even with the good land he must be having a rough time of it. I've had a good harvest. I think I'll bring him some sheaves of wheat tonight and just leave them in his barn. So he counted out twelve sheaves of wheat and slipped over and left them.

Meanwhile the younger brother was thinking about his older brother: My brother has never married, and he must be lonely without a wife and children. And he got the poorer land. My harvest has been especially good this year. I think I'll take some sheaves of wheat over to him and just leave them in his barn. He counted out twelve sheaves of wheat and slipped over in the darkness and left them in the barn. Both brothers went to bed feeling very good.

The next morning they were both in their barns counting sheaves, and they couldn't figure out how they had given away twelve sheaves and yet still seemed to have them. They both decided to bring more. So that night they counted out twelve more sheaves and added in a jar of olives, and they slipped past each other in the dark and left them in the barns. Again the third morning they were counting, and they found that what they had given away they still had. Once more they counted out twelve sheaves, a jar of olives and now they added new wine. That night each took his donkey and set out for the other's barn.

But this night the moon was full and they met halfway, at the border of their lands. When they realized what each was doing, they fell into each others arms weeping, remembering their father and praising God. They promised from that day forward not to forget and to stay together.

The Jews say that the spot where the brothers met is the spot that the elders of the Jewish community chose for the building of the Temple in Jerusalem, for wherever brothers meet is holy ground and God is worshiped and glorified. Today, when the story is told, it is said that at any border where brothers, sisters, families, neighbors, nations and enemies meet is the temple, is holy ground, and that God is delighted and peace comes to earth.

9

The Compassionate One

———— ■ ————

Jesus had made up his mind to go to Jerusalem, the pivotal point of all of his journeys in Luke's gospel, and he had sent messengers ahead of him to find lodging. But the people of the Samaritan village wouldn't receive him, because he was on his way to Jerusalem. The old enmities went deep between the Jews and the Samaritans. James and John, aptly named the sons of thunder, responded to the villagers' inhospitality by asking Jesus: "Lord, do you want us to call down fire from heaven to reduce them to ashes?" Jesus rebuked them, and they moved on to another village (Luke 9:51-56). Interestingly enough this chapter and the next are both about hospitality, welcoming the message and the bearers of the good news and being sent as missionaries and preachers out into the world. They are about how to travel, whom to travel with, how to be a visitor, and knowing when it is time to go or stay. It is in this context that we read the famous story of our neighbor: the good Samaritan, who is unnamed but well-remembered.

This story follows a pattern that Luke uses often; it is a story within a story within a story, much like his famous three "lost" stories—the lost coin, the lost sheep and the lost child. Those stories say something on their own, but their true power lies in their intricate interweaving and especially in the context of their audience and how they end.

To introduce the story of the good Samaritan, let me re-count another story.

■ Once upon a time there was a king. He was a good king, just and careful in his realm. But his real passion was to be the best archer in the whole world. He began with a simple bow and arrow made by his father. With much practice he became adept. By the time he was in his late teens he could hit the bull's-eye about 50 percent of the time. But for him that was not good enough. He sent out a message through all his kingdom that he wanted a teacher, a master to train him and better his marksmanship, and so for years he studied with the best in the land. His percentage of hitting the bull's-eye improved remarkably—to 75 or 80 percent. Still it was not good enough.

Word of his passion spread beyond his own kingdom's borders, and one day a master from a far land arrived and said he would help him. Much to the king's surprise, the man did not concentrate on form, or the quality of his bow and arrows, or the king's stance, or even his strength or coordination. Instead he approached the issue from a totally different angle. He taught the king to concentrate, to center himself and to close his eyes before letting the arrow go toward the target! The king was dubious but obedient, and to his surprise, over the weeks and months, his aim improved. He could hit the bull's-eye more than 85 percent of the time.

Then, at the master's insistence, he began to think of himself as the arrow and as the bow—one with the target. To everyone's amazement he improved still more. But his accuracy stopped at 90 percent or so. He was stuck there. And yet his dream was to hit the bull's-eye 100 percent of the time.

Years passed, and he went about his duties as king. One day as he was out riding in a small, out-of-the-way village he spied a number of bull's-eyes drawn on the side of a barn. Amazingly, every single one of them had an arrow dead center! As he continued to ride through the small village, it seemed every building had a number of targets, and every single one of them was centered with an arrow.

The king was elated. Here was the teacher who would help him master his bow and his mind. The king stopped and asked and found to his surprise that the master archer was a young man, only twelve years old. The king sought him out and shared his hope with him, and immediately the young boy said he would teach the king.

Off they went to find a barn. The two stood at a good distance from the building, and the boy proceeded to tell the king how to stand, how to hold the bow, how to flock his arrow, how to look at the target, even how to breathe. And the king obeyed. Then the boy told him to take aim, breathe deeply, and let the arrow fly. The king took aim at the barn but then stopped. He turned toward the boy and said, "But there is no target." And the boy smiled at him and said: "I know. That's the best part. After you let your arrow go, you paint the target around the arrow." That was how the boy always hit the mark dead center!

This story is a bit annoying. We feel cheated, taken in, set up, even made fun of. I suspect that this was exactly how the young lawyer felt when Jesus told his good neighbor story. It has a bit of the same flavor, the same dissatisfaction and the same disorientation. The prelude to the story is loaded:

■ *Then a teacher of the Law came and began putting Jesus to the test. And he said, "Master, what shall I do to receive eternal life?" Jesus replied, "What is written in the Scripture? How do you understand it?" The man answered, "It is written: You shall love the Lord your God with all your heart and all your soul, with all your strength and with all your mind. And you shall love your neighbor as yourself." Jesus replied, "What a good answer! Do this and you shall live."*

The man wanted to keep up appearances, so he replied, "Who is my neighbor?" The lawyer is out to test Jesus, to set him up, much as an enemy sets out to trip his opponent. He knows the Law—is on his own turf—and wants Jesus to validate his own perceptions and answers. And Jesus does! He compliments him with the words: "What a good answer! Do this and you shall live!" Jesus uses the lawyer's own words to put in a nutshell what is necessary for eternal life: loving God with all the fullness of our being and loving our neighbor. The words of the Law, the Torah, the testament of the Jews hold the kernels of truth, and Jesus turns them back toward the lawyer, adding: "Do this and you shall live!" This is eternal life *now*—given, not expected and waited for, but capable of being received, grasped and held even now. If you want to live forever now, then do this: love God with all your heart and all your soul and all your mind and love your neighbor as yourself.

The lawyer doesn't seem to have any trouble with the God part; he seems to believe that he does love God with all his heart and soul and mind. It is the other part that disturbs him a bit. He is a lawyer, after all, so he wants Jesus to be specific about who his neighbor is. That is the open door, the crack that Jesus uses to step in and shatter the man's entire existence and structure of belief and perception. He tells the Jewish lawyer a story:

■ *There was a man going down from Jerusalem to Jericho, and he fell into the hands of robbers. They stripped him, beat him and went off leaving him half dead.*

It happened that a priest was going along that road and saw the man, but passed by on the other side. Likewise a Levite saw the man and passed by on the other side. But a Samaritan, too, was going along that road, and when he come upon the man, he was moved with compassion. He went over to him and treated his wounds with oil and wine and wrapped them with bandages. Then he put him on his own animal and brought him to an inn where he took care of him.

The next day he had to set off, but gave two silver coins to the innkeeper and told him: "Take care of him and whatever you spend on him, I will repay when I come back."

Jesus then asked, "Which of these three, do you think, made himself neighbor to the man who fell into the hands of robbers?" The teacher of the Law answered, "The one who had mercy on him." And Jesus said, "Go then and do the same" (Luke 10:30-36).

This is a classic story, much like a teaching story from any religious tradition, where the teacher tells the story, then turns the question back to the students or questioners. The word *question* comes from the shorter word *quest*, meaning "to search out," "to go on a journey." Jesus takes the lawyer on a journey, a quest beyond the reaches of his belief, the parameters of his compassion and shoves him over the limit. And the lawyer answers and is caught. It is the style of the rabbi, the master, the guru to use our questions to stand us on our head or pull the rug out from under us, sometimes gently, sometimes roughly, but always with the truth.

Sometimes we don't immediately see the connection between the lawyer's initial response about loving God and our neighbor with Jesus' story of the good Samaritan. What is Jesus saying? In his mind and heart the lawyer has separated God from his neighbor. He wants some limits and boundaries set on whom he has to love.

And what about the inner story—the man traveling by himself, coming back from Jerusalem? He is a Jew, so no matter what business he was about in Jerusalem, he would have taken the opportunity to stop at the Temple and worship. Now he has been beaten, stripped and left for dead— without human dignity and without identity. He is anybody and nobody, a victim of random violence.

Then there is the lawyer—what do we know of him? He is clearly articulate, astute. He is trying to understand so that he can apply the Law. He is aware that just knowing the Law doesn't necessarily mean a person lives it. He has the right answer to his question; he has eternal life if he practices it. Are we like this lawyer? Do we love God and feel secure in that, yet see the issue as the neighbor and what we have to do in that regard? God is within, the neighbor is without.

The lawyer knows the Law but has no sense of his own sinfulness, self-righteousness, reluctance to fulfill his obligations. Daily he would have drawn his prayer shawl around himself and prayed. When questioned by Jesus he has the right answer, but acting upon his knowledge is another matter. Jesus tells him explicitly, "Go then and do the same." Does he? Do we? The lawyer, the teacher of the Law, says to Jesus that his neighbor is not just the Jew, as the Law specifies, but the one in need or, more to the point, the one who treats even his enemy with compassion and mercy. His understanding of the Law has been expanded and deepened.

The bull's-eye has been drawn around him, specifically. He knows now that his neighbor is the last person in the world he'd want near him! Maybe this lawyer went out and lived what was demanded of him, and maybe he went out and joined the plot to kill Jesus and leave him for dead, outside the city of Jerusalem. Or maybe he sought again to justify himself. We don't know.

What is the Jesus of this story like? He's sharp, tough, challenging; he successfully plays word games with the lawyer. He makes his point and wins the case hands down. Jesus tells a story that the lawyer must accept, and yet the story undermines the lawyer's whole present reality. More important, it undermines the notion of using the Law to *keep* from doing justice to our neighbor. Jesus puts the two prongs of the Law together as one: love of God is love of our neighbor, and to love God we must love our neighbor, our enemy, our unknown strangers with all our heart and soul and mind. If we do that, we live. If not, we are dead, notwithstanding our place in the synagogue, school, law, society, community. Jesus is hard; he takes the things that this man holds dear and fast and says no! this is not how things operate in my kingdom.

What of the Samaritan that Jesus singles out as the good neighbor, the image of those who love God with all their heart and soul and mind? The Jews detested the Samaritans, having no dealings with them. The Jews considered them heretical, a sect that had separated from Judaism, tending more toward the worship and traditions of the patriarchs rather than the Law and the prophets. They even worshiped on a different mountain. It was a racial, religious and nationalistic hatred that was taken very personally as well as communally. For a Jew to call someone a Samaritan was a high insult, degrading. How did the man in the ditch, the good Jew, feel when he woke up and found that he had been nursed and cared for by a Samaritan, and that the man was coming back to repay the innkeeper? What does he do? Would he rather have died than have a Samaritan take care of him? How can he face his community knowing all its taboos and laws have been breached? Now he owed the Samaritan his life, and further, he was ritually unclean.

In fact, the Jew rescued from the ditch is in the same position as the lawyer. He is faced with a dilemma and a decision that will forever alter his quest and his life. The question posed to us is this: If we were in a ditch in that condition, who is the last person in the world we'd want to help us, the last person we would want to be indebted to for the rest of our lives, especially if acknowledging the debt would cause us to be outcast and associated with that group by everyone in our current world? Is there anyone or any group that we feel that way about? Would we rather die than face the fact that this person or these people are our neighbors? Perhaps they live eternal life now, while we are spiritually dead.

And what about this Samaritan? He has money; he has oil, wine, a donkey or animal, some beast of burden. He also has a good reputation, because the innkeeper trusts him or he is a regular customer and makes the trip often. He takes a chance and helps this anonymous stranger; "he is moved to pity by the sight of the stripped, beaten and left for dead man" (*NAB*). He is courageous and unselfish and practices the corporal works of mercy as needed with no qualms about whom he is helping or whether it is convenient. This unknown man's needs change the Samaritan's journey, interrupting his work and his life as he practices hands-on justice.

If this were a one-time story it wouldn't be impossible for us to rise to the occasion. But if this is reality, enduring and constant, then to do so we need friends. Part of eternal life is making sure our friends are the friends of God, like the innkeeper and the Samaritan, so that those who minister can pick up the slack. Words of belief and religion are validated by the community, and works of mercy and justice must be practiced continually, personally and collectively in everyday life. We are to make ourselves good neighbors to all, even going far out of our way to respond to immediate needs for survival and justice.

There are still others in the story. The priest and the Levite see what has happened and pass on by for their own reasons. The route is a dangerous one, and they have their own reasons for choosing it: necessity, time, destination, even ministry. They are on their way, heading away from Jerusalem. Sometimes we are hard on the priest, but knowing some of the background of the priesthood in the Jewish community may put his actions in perspective.

At the time of Jesus, many priests took turns by lot at performing the rituals of sacrifice in the Temple. A man would wait all his life for perhaps one turn, one chance to perform what gave meaning to his entire life and position in the tribe of priests. When he was called forth by lot he had to prove himself clean, worthy and in a position to offer the sacrifice. If he had touched anyone with blood or a dead person, he would defile himself and be unable to offer the sacrifice, and his turn would pass on to another. He had everything to lose by stopping. The demands of ritual purification, of the Law and of society demanded that he pass by.

The Levite was in the same position, although not as drastic perhaps. If he touched the man, he too would be subject to a period of purification and separation from the community. He would not be able to perform his duties, his paid professional services to the priests and the people for that period of time. He would inconvenience himself and lose income, connections and participation in the life of the Temple. So he saw and passed by as well.

The lifestyles and ministries and place within the existing religious structure for the priest and the Levite mitigated against personal works of mercy and justice. They had much to lose in stepping off the road. They see but are not moved to pity or to action. They move along, rationalize, and go on with their personal lives. They do not get involved. They go their way. The way of Jesus is the way to the Father, the way of the cross, the way of justice, the way into the kingdom. Instead, they go their own way, not the way of Jesus or the way of the cross or the way to eternal life. They go away from the kingdom, away from pity and compassion, away from touching another person's distress, away from unconditional risks for a stranger and enemy. As Martin Luther King, Jr., stated in regard to this text:

> To begin with, we must be the good Samaritan to those who have fallen along the way. This, however, is only the beginning. Then, some day we will necessarily have to realize that the road to Jericho must be made in such a way that men and women are not constantly beaten and robbed while they are traveling along the paths of life.

Jesus points out, albeit with subtlety, that those in power religiously or otherwise may know the Law but may not put it into practice at the service of those who need it, which is the only reason for the existence of the Law and those who study and promulgate the Law. Jesus knows that the Jews believe the Law imposes an obligation in relation to other Jews, but Jesus is adamant that the Law is the lowest common denominator for our behavior toward all human beings.

Perhaps at this point something should be said about the robbers. These thieves are violent, organized perhaps, and willing to prey upon anyone who passes by. The road to Jericho was known to be dangerous; the story is told in the context of violence and thievery, the reality of life. Eternal life happens along the way of violence and robbery, the way we travel in our own destinies and ministries.

The Law says: Do this and you shall live; be compassionate toward all those in need and you will live; otherwise you will be dead even now. The lawyer listening to the story did not go away feeling justified. Mere appearances won't work with Jesus. We must offer wholehearted, single-minded compassion. It is worth noting that the only other time Jesus says the words *do this* is at the Last Supper: "Do this and remember me." This is a story not just about the Law and about loving God and our neighbor. It is about true worship. *Do this*: Be compassionate and then we may take the bread of compassion at Eucharist with our whole soul and mind and heart. Being compassionate toward others, making neighbors of all people is the beginning of communion. We become the friends, the companions of God, those who break bread with God when we break open our lives and care for the needs of our neighbors as our God has done with us.

In some translations the Samaritan is described as "being moved to pity for the man in the ditch." *Pity* has many different nuances, and many people resist using the word at all. It has the sense of looking down on someone else, of inequality; it has connotations of degrading and shameful need, of indignity, of being pathetic. No one wants to be pitied, to be put in that kind of position ever, to be treated without personal knowledge and relationship. Whom do we pity? The list seems endless: the homeless, the poor, the handicapped, abused children and old people, the sick, those with

AIDS, prisoners, aliens, those dying of incurable diseases, addicts, those in despair, those without control over their lives. No one wants to be in any of those positions, in that kind of need.

But there is another question to consider: Who pities us? We usually don't think about this question. We don't want to be pitied by anyone, for any reason—except maybe God. God can pity us when we are in need of forgiveness, help, mercy, when we are desperate, alone, sinful, facing death or sickness or injustice. But we want no one else's pity. In fact, being pitied makes us angry and annoyed. Being pitied implies that we are lacking something, in need, perhaps even unaware that we are in such a desperate situation.

Would we rather have God pity us or another person? What can God do for us that our neighbor cannot? If we are left in a ditch, what can God do for us that a person can't do? . . . Yes, the way God pities us is through one another, through those who make themselves our neighbors and love us with all their hearts and souls and minds, as they love themselves and their own life. They get down into the ditch and take care of us without even knowing who we are, because our immediate need is overwhelming. They act as God acts toward us. Pity is close to mercy, the practical corporal works of mercy: feeding the hungry; giving drink to the thirsty; clothing the naked; sheltering the homeless; freeing the imprisoned; taking care of and healing the sick; burying the dead. The Samaritan was *moved* to pity. The Levite and the priest saw but were not moved.

Pity is very specific, depending on the person and the situation: getting into the ditch, pouring oil and wine, lifting him up, taking him to an inn, caring for him, paying for his lodging, sharing his responsibility with the innkeeper, promising to return with more money to pay expenses. It means an ongoing relationship and responsibility and obligation. Jesus is saying that we must be moved to pity by the sight of those in need, the victims of violence, those reduced to indignity and anonymity, those in need of the truth. Jesus is pitying the lawyer just as the Samaritan is pitying the Jew in the ditch, both unconscious of their situation and need. The lawyer must learn to admit that he needs pity before he can be moved with pity on behalf of another. Pity moves us toward our enemies, toward the victims of violence, toward those in the ditch. Pity sets us in motion against injustice, interrupting our lives and journeys and making enemies into friends so that we can live compassionately with them, practicing mercy as a way of life.

God had pity on the human race and sent us Jesus. We are sent to the world to have pity on those in need, to return the favor of God. We are instructed: "Go then, and do the same." Imitate God, imitate the good Samaritan, do what is necessary for others' life, dignity and future. Then we shall love the Lord our God with all our hearts and souls and minds and our neighbor as we love ourselves.

There is a saying among storytellers: The story begins when the teller stops talking. What does the lawyer do when Jesus stops talking? What does the Jew in the ditch do when he awakens in the inn and finds out who has helped him? What does the good Samaritan do when he returns to the inn? What do we do now in response to the Word?

But the story isn't over. There is still another part. It is the story of Mary and Martha and Jesus. We usually look at this story separate from all that has come immediately before in the chapter. But in light of all that has gone before, this short piece about Mary and Martha says something very different from what we are used to hearing.

> As Jesus and his disciples were on their way, he entered a village and a woman called Martha welcomed him to her house. She had a sister named Mary who sat down at the Lord's feet to listen to his words. Martha, meanwhile, was busy with all the serving and finally she said, "Lord, don't you care that my sister has left me to do all the serving?"
>
> But the Lord answered, "Martha, Martha, you worry and are troubled about many things, whereas only one thing is needed. Mary has chosen the better part, and it will not be taken away from her" (Luke 10: 38-42).

In the story of the good Samaritan Jesus is talking about himself. He is on his way to the cross and rejection and persecution and torture, to being stripped and left to die on a garbage dump outside the city. Jesus is going to be the one in the ditch, and there will be many who pass by and see but are not moved to pity because they are busy about many things, intent on their own journeys. He will be buried in a borrowed tomb, and some of the women will watch from a distance. Jesus is saying that whatever we do to the least of our brothers and sisters, we do to him; he knows he soon will be among the least himself. He will be executed legally, though unjustly, tortured horribly, and many will look on.

What then is Jesus saying to Martha? Mary is sitting at Jesus' feet, as a disciple, bending before him, lowering herself. Martha is indignant and asks Jesus to justify her own actions, her own choices in regard to hospitality. It is her house and her meal preparations. It is she who welcomes Jesus inside, off the road. But it is Mary who stops everything and sits at his feet listening, full of personal care, intimate with Jesus.

Jesus does not allow Martha to use him to chastise her sister. That is a breach of hospitality—using a guest to validate or vindicate one's own behavior in regard to a family member. Instead, Jesus defends Mary's actions and choices and tells Martha to leave her alone, that she has chosen the better part, something that is important and crucial for a disciple.

What has Mary chosen? What is Jesus defending? Martha is standing above Jesus. Mary is seated at his feet. Jesus is going to be in the ditch soon. If we are to choose the better part we are to do the corporal works of mercy, to align ourselves with the victims, the oppressed and the needy, with anyone who does the corporal works of mercy. Jesus will die because of the stories he tells and the works he does. He freely goes into the ditch to share that pain and suffering and injustice and violence. Mary is accompanying him there, but Martha is still busy about many things that serve her own ends and life and relationships. Mary is paying attention to Jesus' words, the voice of the oppressed, the prophet's words of justice, the searing words of truth that expose all of humankind's meanness of spirit and selfish intents. Jesus is on his way to Jerusalem, and he needs comfort, presence, touch, intimacy and closeness. This better portion, then, is listening to the victims, giving them strength when they are close to death and so, close to God.

Martha—like the priest and the Levite and the teacher of the Law—doesn't see Jesus and his needs and what he is facing in the near future. Instead she sees her own need, sees her own agenda, and sees Jesus in relation to what she is doing. Mary's point of defiance is that she dares to proclaim what is new in Jesus while Martha is still busy about socially acceptable understandings of hospitality and about what she does best. Mary is in solidarity with Jesus; Martha is firmly attached to society's expectations. Mary does not accept the givens of history; rather, she becomes a disciple, attentive to the presence of the one who is setting his face toward Jerusalem and the cross.

As with the lawyer, Jesus is a conscience to Martha, pointing out the privilege of discipleship and singling out Mary as one who has made herself neighbor to the one in need. Mary is pitying Jesus and acting out of compassion, putting herself at the feet of the kingdom, at the service of those in the midst of pain, struggle and hope, in jeopardy with the victims and those who devote themselves to the cause of justice. This is to choose the better part: God's part in siding with those we disdain, ignore and do not think are worth our time, our risk, our compassion and mercy.

This set of parables is about our neighbors. And so, who after all are our neighbors? Our neighbors are those in need of compassion. Our neighbors are those who are the victims of injustice, violence, robbery, who are placed or find themselves in life-threatening positions, stripped of dignity. Our neighbors are those who need ongoing commitments from us and others besides us to get them back on the way, back to normal lives. Our neighbors are those who reveal God: outsiders, ditch folk, "Samaritans," enemies, other races, heretics, criminals. Our neighbors are those who befriend the poor, speak out against injustice, do mercy, critique the system and, inevitably, join the victims in the ditch. Our neighbors are those who do not validate our behaviors and choices and reasoning but challenge us to change, look again and not use our religion to manipulate our reality into a better position or place with God. Our neighbors are those who remind us forcibly that society's givens do not help those most in need and sometimes create the environment that produces as many victims as there are those who can take advantage of the system. Our neighbors are the painful, frightening presences who remind us of the violence, lawlessness and hate in our society and who afford us the chance to bring hope into those situations.

Perhaps this parable should be renamed the parable of the good neighbor, or the parable of the compassionate one, or the parable of the one who loves God wholeheartedly, or even the parable of the better portion. For this parable is about Jesus, the Compassionate One who sees rightly and judges justly because he himself suffers unjustly, an innocent victim at the hands of people (Isaiah 50).

Often this story of Mary and Martha is used to delineate the differences between active and contemplative life, with contemplative life being, naturally, the better portion. But there are ways to look at this portion of the gospel with some major shifts of focus and concentration.[1]

The story does provide us with stages of hospitality in choosing the option for the poor or obeying the fundamental imperative of the gospel as well as in living the way of contemplation. Contemplation is sometimes seen as a long, loving look at reality. The first stage of commitment to the poor and the first stage of prayer are looking, seeing the situation, and knowing and being moved to compassion. They result in doing the works of mercy, hands-on justice. They discover that pity is both the sight of reality that makes us ill and the response of anger that sets in motion something altogether new.

The second stage of both commitment to the poor and contemplation lies in a gradual discovery that no matter how many times we get into the ditch, no matter how many singular acts of mercy we do, it is the system and the structures

---

[1]Some of the following ideas evolved from suggestions by Albert Nolan, O.P., a theologian who has written a number of articles on solidarity, the poor, and liberation theology, including "The Service of the Poor and Spiritual Growth," Justice Papers No. 6, 1985. Catholic Institute for International Relations, London.

that perpetuate the misery and contribute to the violence. Society keeps adding to the victims, stripping people of self-worth and value by laws and attitudes, robbing, beating and leaving many half-dead in the ditch. It is structural injustice and violence that are the root causes of individual problems. This is the dark night of the senses and purgation, which results in a lifestyle and spirituality that is made of the acts of mercy, asceticism, shared suffering and pain with the disease of others. It means reaching out to touch that person; it means forgetting self and consciously separating ourselves from the structures that cause so much inhumanity to others.

This awareness of the enormity of evil, of sin and its structural as well as individual character leads to another kind of anger and rage: the prophet's rage. And it leads into the dark night of the soul: the recognition of the nearness of evil, the enormity of the struggle and the terrible price of dignity, liberation and salvation.

Yet this is also illumination and the choice to accompany, the choice to get into the ditch and stay with the victims. It is the time to push our own privilege, as Mary did, and speak truth on behalf of those who have no voice and walk with and break bread with them. It is the choice to sit at the feet of the poor, with Jesus. This is the better part: to become a disciple with Jesus, who will be left to die as a criminal on a hill outside the city.

This choice makes one a prophet publicly or privately, seeing and knowing sin and yet seeing at the same time that it is the victims of evil who will save us all. They are more capable than we are of standing in opposition to evil and sin because they have experienced its power in their own flesh and lives. This choice begins a deep conversion to humility, a call to serve others in body and soul with our own weaknesses, lacks and failures, our own poverty. It is a choice to stand outside, against oppression, and begin to bear the cross within our own flesh on behalf of and with others who have no choice. It is an enduring way, a commitment to the way of the cross, a faithful acceptance of the ditch, and awareness that God lies in the ditch with the victims.

Resurrection life is a pledge of life as an act of hope that makes us one both with God and our neighbors. It can have moments of ecstasy as with Mary, and hard moments between family and friends as with Martha. It can have confrontative moments as with Jesus and the lawyer, and moments of insight and critique of the system, as with Jesus using the priest and the Levite to show how the religious structure can ignore the moment of God breaking into and interfering with our schedules and so revealing our lack of love and mercy and our lack of knowledge of what true religion is. This is the way of discipleship, the way of contemplation and the way of embracing the fundamental imperative of the gospel. This is the way the kingdom comes: in mercy, in compassion and love, in siding with the ditch folk, with Jesus, with the scriptures that call us to obey the presence of God in our midst. If we do this, then we will know resurrection life, life eternal even now.

This is the way of hospitality, of making space for God and others in our lives, of making the world and the earth a more habitable place to live. It is the way of putting ourselves out so that others may enter into the kingdom.

A final story reminds us of the depth and extent to which Jesus practiced this parable himself and calls us to practice it with him. It is a story from the Hindu tradition, and it is called "The Guru and the Mantra of Life and Death."

■ Once upon a time there was a teacher, a guru who had many followers. They came from all over to listen, to learn wisdom and enlightenment and to be liberated from their desires and needs. There were classes and one-on-one apprenticeships. At the end of the students' teaching the master would send them out into the world to share their learning and knowledge with others as masters in their own right. And just before they left, he would give them a gift: the mantra of life and death. Phrase by phrase he would teach them until they had learned it by heart. Then he would tell them that as long as they said this mantra faithfully, they would be blessed; that its power would give them insight and clarity and allow them to discern the truth when all around them were lies and shadows; that its power would keep them from despair and give them hope in the midst of misery and hopelessness; that its power would strengthen their faith and one day save their souls and give them everlasting life. The disciples were grateful and humbled by the gift. Then he warned them never to teach anyone else the mantra; it was for them alone, those who had been enlightened.

And so for years and years students finished their studies, were given the mantra and went out into the world to share their wisdom and to pray their mantra in secret. One day a young man came to the master, ready to go into the world. He too was taught the mantra and humbled by the enormity of the gift that he was given. However, when the master warned him not to share the mantra with anyone, he asked why. The master looked long and hard at him: "If you share this mantra with others, then what it was to do for you will be handed over to them. And you will live in darkness even when the light is all around you. You will know only despair and misery of body and soul all your life. You will stumble over the truth and be confused endlessly. Worst of all, you will lose your faith, and you will lose your soul. You will be dammed forever."

The disciple turned white and shook visibly and nodded and left the master's presence. But he was troubled in spirit. Finally, he decided what he had to do. He went to the nearest large city and gathered the multitudes about him, teaching and enthralling them with his stories and wisdom. Then he taught them the mantra, line by line, phrase by phrase, just as his master had taught him. There was a hush, and people left whispering the mantra to themselves.

A number of the master's disciples were in the crowd, and they were horrified at the man's actions. He had disobeyed the master. He had betrayed his community. He had given away the wisdom and the gift to the ignorant and unenlightened. They immediately went back to the master and told him what had happened.

They asked him: "Master, are you going to punish him for what he has done?" The master looked at them sadly and said: "I do not have to. He will be punished terribly. He knew what his fate would be if he shared the mantra of life with those who were not enlightened. For him it has become the mantra of death. He will live in darkness and despair, without hope or knowledge of the truth. He will live isolated, alone, without comfort or faith, and he will die terribly and lose even his own soul. How could I possibly punish him? He knew what he was choosing." And with those words, the old master rose and gathered his few belongings and began to walk away. "Master," one disciple asked, "where are you going?" And the master looked at all of them sadly and spoke, "I am going to that man who gave away my gift of the mantra of life and death." "Why?" they chorused. "Because," he said, "out of all my students, he alone learned wisdom and compassion. Now that man is my master." And he left them to follow the man who walked now in darkness and despair, who had chosen compassion over wisdom and knowledge.

Our God broke all the laws, shattered all the boundaries and turned over all the understandings of religion, of obedience and of love in sending us the Compassionate One, Jesus of Nazareth, the Crucified One who is the mantra of life and death. This choice of compassion and pity is what opens the door to resurrection and hope. It is the better part. And nothing can take it away from those who have been touched by the mercy of God.

10

Jesus, the Last Arrow and the Archer

■

John's gospel begins with time before time: In the beginning was the Word and the Word was with God and the Word was God; he was in the beginning with God (John 1:1-2). This, of course, is the incarnation, the mystery of God becoming human, the Word becoming flesh and blood and dwelling among us forever. It is the core, the heart of our religion, our belief and our meaning as followers of Jesus. Jesus is all we know of God in humankind, in flesh and blood and bone.

Jesus is the revelation of God, Lord to the glory of God the Father in the power of the Holy Spirit. Jesus is the entrance, the doorway, the icon into the Trinity, the community of God. Jesus is the suffering servant, the one rejected even by his own followers and friends.

Jesus is the poor man, without a place to lay his head and at the last, without even the face and form of humankind, but "a worm and no man" because of the violence and hatred that he experienced from others. Jesus, son of Mary is also Son of Man and Sun of Justice, manchild, helpless, hunted as a babe and persecuted as an adult. Jesus is the parable of God: unexpected, unbelievable, unfathomable except by love, single-minded and single-hearted in revealing to us our fathering God, the forgiving, reconciling, merciful and just God. Jesus is driven by the Spirit to speak only the truth, calling us to conversion, transformation, the favor of God and graceful living, calling us to be human, to be words of God by, in our turn, forgiving, restoring, doing restitution, repairing the world, encouraging and giving hope and speaking a word that heartens and draws forth life even in the face of despair and death, sin and evil.

Jesus is the parable of God. John's gospel contains only one parable, sometimes called the parable of the apprentice, for it describes Jesus as the apprentice of God.

> Jesus said to them, "Truly, I assure you, the Son cannot do anything by himself, but only what he sees the *Father* do. And whatever he does, the Son also does. The *Father* loves the Son and shows him everything he does; and he will show him even greater things than these, so that you will be amazed.
>
> As the *Father* raises the dead and gives them life, so the Son gives life to whom he wills. In the same way the *Father* judges no one, for he has entrusted all judgment to the Son, and he wants all to honor the Son as they honor the *Father*. Whoever ignores the Son, ignores as well the *Father* who sent him.
>
> Truly, I say to you, he who hears my word and believes him who sent me, has eternal life; and there is no judgment for him because he has passed from death to life.
>
> Truly, the hour is coming and has indeed come, when the dead will hear the voice of the Son of God and, on hearing it, will live. For the *Father* has life in himself and he has given to the Son also to have life in himself. And he has empowered him as well to carry out Judgment, for he is a son of man" (John 5:19-27).

So Jesus is an apprentice, imitating the God that he sees and knows and in so doing revealing this God, his Father, to all who see and know and come to believe in him. To see Jesus is to see God. To hear the stories of God leads to the story of God: Jesus, Son of the Father, Son of Man and son of man. The term *son of man* was oftentimes used as a simple description in the Jewish community for a human being; it is the term that Jesus uses most often to describe himself to his followers.

Jesus is the one who judges justly because he himself has suffered unjustly at the hands of all people. The work of judgment, the bringing of justice, of balance and harmony to the broken world and broken-hearted people is the work of this human being, Jesus, the revelation of God. And so it is the work of all human beings, made holy and full of grace by Jesus' presence, passion and pity among us and for us even until now. Jesus does only what he sees the Father doing: healing, curing, forgiving, telling the truth to power, being nonviolent, making peace, reconciling, welcoming the stranger and the Samaritan, embracing the leper and the sinner and the outcast, recasting and reforming them into the image of God's chosen ones, beloved and adopted as children into this entirely new family and creation that Jesus sets in motion by his appearance upon earth and keeps spreading through those who believe in him and reveal his presence still among us in the least of our brothers and sisters.

And there will be even greater things than this: greater than the lame leaping up like deer and dancing; greater than the blind seeing and the deaf hearing; greater than the good news being preached and hope being given to the poor of the earth; greater than prisoners set free and captives liberated; greater than forgiveness in the face of betrayal and selfishness and insensitivity and self-righteousness; greater than feeding all those who hunger and thirst for food and justice and human dignity. Still greater than all this is the resurrection, the most amazing work of the Father, catching his beloved child in his arms as he falls in death and raising him from the dead and standing behind him in the world forever. This greatest work is begun in us at baptism and continues to mature and develop throughout our lives, throughout all the history of the world and creation and will come to completion, to justice's end, to wholeness and grace when all shall be judged and revealed in truth and made anew. Now we are the children of God. What we shall be then . . . is yet to be revealed.

We are the beloved children of God by our baptism, our initiation into the kingdom of the Father and Jesus in the Spirit, the kingdom of God, and as Jesus solemnly assures us, we will do the things that he does and we will do even

greater things. We too will heal, reconcile, forgive, do justice, gather into our heart and community, do the works of
mercy and worship our Father with Jesus in the Spirit's grace.
We too will raise the dead and resurrect hope and forgiveness, life ever more abundantly, especially for those most in
need of it: sinners, those who do evil, those who betray their
belief by their behavior and lack of commitment, those who
are dead, without hope and passion, without compassion and
tender regard for others and the earth. We reveal the face of
God and redeem the bodies and hearts and souls of others
by imitating the works of Jesus and being apprentices to the
Father, who Jesus reveals now through our humanity and
obedience.

Jesus speaks of a time, an hour that is coming and has indeed already come. Traditionally, this hour was the hour of
salvation, the hour of crucifixion and death, the hour of passion, when Jesus revealed the depth of his passionate love
for God and his unbounded trust and devotion to his Father,
forgiving those who murdered him, followed orders, rejected
him, betrayed him and went about their usual daily business in the face of injustice, inhumanity and the crying need
for truth and communion. The cross is the way the kingdom
comes. The cross is power in this group of human beings.
The cross is the mark of belonging to God. The cross is what
stretches us outward toward other human beings and opens
a space inside us for God, rooting us in earth and pointing
us toward the heavens. All comes together in the cross: history, judgment, the search for divinity, the quest of being human. The cross contains what is still to be revealed: the mystery of wholeness and full communion with God for all human beings, the garden, the city, the place where the dawn
wipes all tears from our eyes and waters the soil and brings
forth trees and fruit as medicine and even timid lambs lie
down in peace with lions.

Jesus is the storyteller, the parable maker, the one who
turns upside down the image of God: from dominance to
justice and tender-hearted mercy, from warrior-king to
widow in search of her rights, from the singular God of the
chosen people to the God who chooses all peoples, especially
the poor and the cast-aways and the lost sheep, the ones who

wandered away from society and fell into the cracks of structures and were exiled from nations and persecuted by governments and institutions. This parable maker told the stories of God, fiercely repeating and conjuring and imagining new ways to see and appreciate his God—Father; impossibly faithful and hounding widow; vineyard owner, who pays everyone the same and makes the hardy and the best wait the longest; the Samaritan; the enemy in the ditch; the least of our brothers and sisters, who are the most in jeopardy of all human beings. This is the face of Jesus' God. And so Jesus casts in his lot with the least, with those in the ditch, with the unjustly executed ones who knew no mercy from the state and no compassion from their friends. Jesus becomes the suffering servant, the crucified one, the reed broken in the wind, the word silenced, the cry reaching to God that shatters all history and alters the human race forever.

Now humanity is judged by Jesus' presence hidden still in our midst. Now we are called to worship and to honor God by being human, just, merciful and compassionate, nonviolent, embracing our enemies and making friends of strangers and aliens. We are to be words of God, children of God, brothers and sisters to Jesus, driven by the Spirit, sent by the Father, missioned to repair the world and set loose the power of the resurrection shared with us in the story that seems never to end and to grow more unbelievable with each telling. Our God became human so that we would know what it is to be God. The Word was made flesh so that all our flesh might become words that echo and speak of the goodness of God.

Jesus is the arrow hidden in the quiver. No one could have dreamed of this Jesus, the archer of God, and every word, every gesture goes straight to the heart, to every heart. Jesus, the parable of God, reminds us that no matter what we think God is, no matter how sure we are of God, be careful. Maybe we don't know God at all. Maybe there is much more, but we can only learn it by staking our life on this story and throwing in our lot with those who become the story and enchant all the others with its power and grace. Jesus tells us that this story, the story of God, comes true when we do too.

There must be a closing story! It is a story that actually happened in the Jewish community when the Romans ruled Israel in the first century and were intent on eradicating Judaism. They made rules and regulations including not teaching the Torah, not ordaining rabbis and not gathering to pray. The penalty for any infraction was death, and many disobeyed the laws of Yahweh and obeyed instead the laws of Rome in fear and desperation and despair.

■ There was a rabbi, Rabbi Hananiah ben Teradion, who lived in Siknin, a small village in Galilee. He ran a school and taught and prayed in public and refused to obey any of the rules of the Romans. He became famous because of his passionate devotion to the poor and those in need and persecuted. Eventually Reb Hananiah was arrested and sentenced to be burned at the stake. The next day he appeared in the square carrying the Torah scrolls. When confronted by the Romans, he said, "I do only what God commands me." The Romans were furious and so, both to make fun of him and to make his suffering more intense, they took the scrolls of the Torah and wrapped him in them. The long pieces of parchment swaddled his body, and next to his heart they packed wet wool, so that he would live longer through the pain and burning. Then they set the fire with willow wood and watched him die.

His disciples and students gathered around in horror and silence and could do nothing. His daughter stood agonizing and watched. Finally she spoke to her father in grief. But her father answered her, "If I had to die alone, that would have been terrible, but I die now with the scrolls of the Torah, with my beloved words of God, and when God does justice he will remember that I died with his word burning all around me and in my heart." The flames seemed so slow and his pain was awful, but his disciples noticed that the rabbi seemed to be looking at something intently. They asked him, "Rabbi, what do you see?" And with his dying words he told them, "I see the parchment being burned up, but the words, the letters on the parchment, are not being burned. They are leaping and soaring up to heaven, where they will live forever." And with those words, he died.

The words, the stories of God, the parables of Jesus will live forever, but even more, Jesus, the Word of God, the Parable of God lives forever. We, the children who believe in the story and seek with the power of the Spirit to make the story come true for others, are offered a place in that kingdom where we live forever even now in the presence of the Father of Jesus, our Father and God. The community, the trinity expands, the kingdom is coming and who knows what arrows are left, hidden still in the quiver? Who knows what arrows are even now being sent to the heart of the people by the Archer of God, who is always true in his aim and always justly strikes home with the word.

Postscript

———— ■ ————

There are many parables of Jesus that are not in this book. There are very specific reasons for that. Basically the choice is simple: I don't understand some of the others. They are problems to be solved, holes still to fall into and texts to be dug into with others in community. The ones included are gifts from communities that struggle with the scripture and the works of mercy and justice. They are shovels that have opened up deep underground vaults and alerted me to the fact that studying the scriptures for information does not necessarily lead to conversion or understanding of their depth or allow God in Jesus' Spirit to challenge us to become holy and compassionate.

Even as I was writing this book other parables opened up and caught me off guard, adding more pieces to the puzzle of how parables work. These also reveal my own cultural blindness, which works against my seeing and hearing and taking to heart. So, there are other parables to unearth, like the parables of the ten virgins, the wily manager, the two sons sent to the vineyard, the fig tree, the narrow door, the wedding banquet, the king's son.

This book is only an opening, a crack of the door, an invitation to hard work that I pass on to you. The work and confrontation and delight that have gone into this exegesis and small bit of knowing are a way of life, a way of sitting at the feet of Jesus, the scriptures and the poor, the privileged place of revelation today.

The process of struggling with scripture is hard work. It takes much practice and much love to make the stories come true in us in the world today. Other folks have started the digging and the work. The stories are unearthed and given to us. They are stories to make us all come true.